Intermittent Fasting for Women over 50

The Complete Guide to Discover How to Lose Weight Fast, Increase Energy and Detox your Body – Balance Your Hormones Eating the Foods You Love.

And a BONUS of Week Meal Plan and Delicious Recipes.

COPYRIGHT © 2020

TABLE OF CONTENTS

INTRODUCTION

I f you've read about intermittent fasting but aren't sure if it's right for you, the quick answer is: maybe. As a weight loss and fitness expert, I've been following intermittent fasting for a very time-consuming interval sieving through the science, watching displays with the hundreds of thousands of clients I've drilled, and figuring out what really works and what doesn't.

Intermittent fasting is a diet that alternates periods of eating with periods of not eating. In addition to its power to help you blast through a weight loss plateau and burn fat, there is an extraordinary list of therapeutic benefits:

Protects your brain

When my son, Grant, suffered from a severe traumatic brain injury after being in a hit-and-run accident, I explored everything that could support his recovery. Intermittent fasting combined with a ketogenic diet was an amazing grouping that made a huge difference in helping to heal his brain.

Slows aging

Intermittent fasting mimics caloric restriction, which is the most effective way we know of to surge life span. When you fast, it gives your cells the ability to detox and recycle, so your body can slow down aging and even prevent age-related diseases.

Fights cancer

Studies have shown that fasting can prevent cancer and even slow or stop its progression! It can also kill cancer cells while boosting the immune system.

If the above aren't enough to get you motivated about the possibilities of intermittent fasting, here are some more benefits: It increases insulin sensitivity, decreases the risk of cardiovascular disease, boosts energy, and enhances mental focus.

Some people believe it's not necessarily what you eat but when you eat it that matters. Those who practice intermittent fasting (IF) rave about the weight-loss benefits, improved digestion and mood, and skill to crush sugar cravings.

Intermittent fasting decreases insulin levels and increases human growth hormone, which optimizes your body's ability to burn fat.

And while there are different ways to practice IF - some do the 16:8 methods, where they fast for 16 hours and eat in an eight-hour window, while others do 5:2, where they fast for two days a week and eat normally the other five - many people are confused about what accurately they should eat during their feeding window.

It's true that intermittent fasting gives you a little more freedom to eat what you want.

Since you are typically only sitting down to one or two larger meals, you can eat more calories per meal than you would if you ate three or five meals a day.

However, there are ways to optimize your intermittent fasting for weight loss. Some people make the mistake of eating as much of whatever they want, including processed junk food, during their devouring window. If you eat in a calorie surplus, especially of empty calories and processed food, it will undo all the benefits of fasting.

"For optimal results with intermittent fasting, it's important to continue to drink plenty of water and eat nutrient-dense foods during the feeding times," said by an expert in IF field.

CHAPTER 1:

WHAT IS INTERMITTENT FASTING?

Intermittent Fasting (IF) refers to dietary eating arrays that involve not eating or severely restricting calories for a prolonged period of time. There are many unique subgroups of intermittent fasting each with individual variation in the duration of the fast; some for hours, others for day(s). This has become an extremely popular topic in the science society due to all of the potential benefits on fitness and health that are being discovered.

Fasting, or periods of voluntary abstinence from food has been practiced throughout the world for ages. Intermittent fasting with the ambition of improving health relatively new. Intermittent fasting involves hindering intake of food for a set period of time and does not include any changes to the actual foods you are eating. Presently, the most common IF protocols are a daily 16 hours fast and fasting for a whole day, one or two days per week. Intermittent fasting could be considered a natural eating pattern that humans are built to implement and it traces all the way back to our Paleolithic hunter-gatherer ancestors.

The current model of a planned program of intermittent fasting could potentially help improve many aspects of health from body configuration to longevity and aging. Although IF goes against the norms of our culture and common daily routine, the science may be pointing to less meal frequency and more time fasting as the optimal alternative to the normal breakfast, lunch, and dinner model. Here are two common myths that pertain to intermittent fasting.

Myth 1 - You Must Eat 3 Meals Per Day: This "rule" that is common in Western society was not developed based on evidence for improved health, but was adopted as the common pattern for settlers and eventually became the norm. Not only is there a lack of scientific rationale in the 3 meal-a-day model, modern studies may be showing less meals and more fasting to be optimal for human health. One study

3

showed that one meal a day with the same amount of daily calories is better for weight loss and body composition than 3 meals per day. This finding is a basic concept that is extrapolated into intermittent fasting and those choosing to do IF may find it best to only eat 1-2 meals per day.

Myth 2 - You Need Breakfast, It's The Most Important Meal of the Day: Many false claims about the absolute need for a daily breakfast have been made. The most common claims being "breakfast increases your metabolism" and "breakfast decreases food intake later in the day". These claims have been refuted and studied over a 16-week period with results showing that skipping breakfast did not decrease metabolism and it did not increase food intake at lunch and dinner.

It is still feasible to do intermittent fasting protocols while still eating breakfast, but some people find it easier to eat a late breakfast or skip it altogether and this common myth should not get in the way.

Intermittent fasting has become quite the phenomenon these days. Recent studies showed that people who tried it have lost weight, increased health, and believed to have a long existence. Basically, intermittent fasting is a pattern of eating that alternates between periods of fasting, usually consuming only water, and non-fasting, usually eating anything a person want no matter how fattening. In other words, a person can eat anything he wants during a 24-hour period and fast for the next 24 hours.

This methodology to weight control seems to be supported by science, as well as religious and cultural practices around the globe. Adherents of intermittent fasting claim that this practice is a way to become more circumspect about food.

There are many different popular intermittent fasts and hundreds more possible variations. There are two kinds of intermittent fasts that are most basic and frequently used. First is the regular fasting in which the person only gets to eat once every 20-28 hours within a 4-hour period. The second is fasting for 1-3x a week, also called alternate day fasting, in which a person eats anything he wants on one day and fast the whole of next day.

Intermittent fasting has many beneficial effects as tested on animals like rodents and primates. One study found that there has been a "reduced serum glucose and insulin levels and increased resistance of neurons in the brain to excitotoxicity stress". In 2008, a study on intermittent fasting showed that lifespan increases of 40.4% and 56.6% in C. elegance for alternate day (24 hour) and two-of-each-three day (48 hour) fasting, respectively, as compared to an ad libitum diet. And a 2009 study showed that intermittent fasting on rats improved long-term survival after chronic heart failure via pro-angiogenic, anti-apoptotic and anti-remodeling effects.

Scientists caution that only a few studies have been done on humans who are practicing intermittent fasts. The effects of exercise and meal frequency on body composition are an interesting but largely unexplored area of research. However, there are some positive results. Just last month, the Measures of the National Academy of Sciences published a study showing that reducing calories 30% a day increased the memory function of the elderly.

In 2007, the journal Free Radical Biology & Medicine published a study that showed asthma patients who fasted had fewer symptoms, better airway function and a decrease in the markers of inflammation in the blood than those who didn't fast.

Several times have heard from people that Intermittent fasting – isn't that starvation? Lol... it's quit a funny question it's actually a good question to ask before going to (IF)

NO. Fasting differs from starvation in one crucial way: control. Starvation is the involuntary absence of food for a long time, leading to severe suffering or even death. It is neither deliberate nor controlled.

Fasting, on the other hand, is the voluntary withholding of food for spiritual, health, or other reasons. It's done by someone who is not underweight and thus has enough stored body fat to live off. Intermittent fasting done right should not cause suffering, and certainly never death.

Food is easily available, but you choose not to eat it. This can be for any period of time, from a few hours up to a few days or with medical supervision even a week or more. You may begin a fast at any time of your choosing, and you may end a fast at will, too. You can start or stop a fast for any reason or no reason at all.

Fasting has no standard duration, as it is merely the absence of eating.

Anytime that you are not eating, you are intermittently fasting. For example, you may fast between dinner and breakfast the next day, a period of approximately 12-14 hours. In that sense, intermittent fasting should be considered a part of everyday life.

Intermittent fasting is not something queer and curious, but a part of everyday, normal life. It is perhaps the oldest and most powerful dietary intervention imaginable.

Yet somehow we have missed its power and overlooked its therapeutic potential.

Learning how to fast properly gives us the option of using it or not.

At its very core, intermittent fasting simply allows the body to use its stored energy. For example, by burning off excess body fat.

It is imperative to realize that this is normal and humans have evolved to fast for shorter time periods hours or days without detrimental health consequences.

Body fat is merely food energy that has been stored away. If you don't eat, your body will simply "eat" its own fat for energy.

Life is about balance. The good and the bad, the yin and the yang. The same applies to eating and fasting. Fasting, after all, is simply the flip side of eating. If you are not eating, you are fasting.

Here's how it works:

When we eat, more food energy is ingested than can immediately be used. Some of this energy must be stored away for later use. Insulin is the key hormone involved in the storage of food energy.

Insulin rises when we eat, helping to store the excess energy in two separate ways. Carbohydrates are broken down into individual glucose (sugar) units, which can be linked into long chains to form glycogen, which is then stored in the liver or muscle.

There is, however, very limited storage space for carbohydrates; and once that is reached, the liver starts to turn the excess glucose into fat. This process is called de-novo lipogenesis (meaning literally "making new fat").

Some of this newly created fat is stored in the liver, but most of it is exported to other fat deposits in the body. While this is a more complicated process, there is almost no limit to the amount of fat that can be created.

So, two complementary food energy storage systems exist in our bodies. One is easily accessible but with limited storage space (glycogen), and the other is more difficult to access but has almost unlimited storage space (body fat).

The process goes in reverse when we do not eat (intermittent fasting). Insulin levels fall, signaling the body to start burning stored energy as no more is coming through food. Blood glucose falls, so the body must now pull glucose out of storage to burn for energy.

Glycogen is the most easily accessible energy source. It is broken down into glucose molecules to provide energy for the body's other cells. This can provide enough energy to power much of the body's needs for 24-36 hours. After that, the body will primarily be breaking down fat for energy.

So the body only really exists in two states – the fed (insulin high) state and the fasted (insulin low) state. Either we are crediting food energy (increasing stores), or we are burning stored energy (decreasing stores). It's one or the other. If eating and fasting are balanced, then there should be no net weight change.

If we start eating the minute we roll out of bed, and do not stop until we go to sleep, we spend almost all our time in the fed state. Over time, we may gain weight, because we have not allowed our body any time to burn stored food energy.

To restore balance or to lose weight, we may simply need to increase the amount of time spent burning food energy.

That's intermittent fasting.

In essence, intermittent fasting allows the body to use its stored energy. After all, that's what it is there for. The important thing to understand is that there is nothing wrong with that. That is how our bodies are designed. That's what dogs, cats, lions and bears do. That's what humans do.

If you are eating every third hour, as is often optional, then your body will constantly use the incoming food energy. It may not need to burn much body fat, if any. You may just be storing fat.

Your body may be saving it for a time when there is nothing to eat.

If this happens, you lack balance. You lack intermittent fasting.

HOW OUR MODERN DIET IS A PROBLEM?

It's no undisclosed that obesity is on the rise in our country.

Right now, more than one-third of all adults in the U.S. are obese, totaling a whopping 78.6 million. But obesity isn't just a problem; it's downright dangerous to the population.

Obesity raises the risk of a whole slew of unwanted health conditions, like heart disease, diabetes, stroke and even some kinds of cancer. In fact, it's actually the leading cause of preventable death in our country.

Sadly, with the modern diet the way it is, it's no surprise our society has this problem. In the last few decades, the types of food we eat as well as the amounts of food have changed dramatically. Foods are more processed, they're fried into handy, to-go packages, and they're served up in super-sized portions.

Let's take a deeper look at the modern diet, and how it's led our country's health astray.

Today's diet is drastically diverse than that of Americans just 30 or 40 years ago. Then, most food was fresh, grown nearby, and cooked at home. Now, almost everything you buy has been processed even the stuff you plan to cook at home! It comes with additives, chemicals, colorings, sugars, trans fats and tons of other ingredients you wouldn't have found just a generation or two ago.

Additionally, the consumption of sugar has risen dramatically over the past couple of decades, and the average American now consumes a shocking 22 teaspoons of sugar a day, or 25 percent of their daily caloric intake. That's up 10 percent from just 10 years ago, and 20 percent since 1970.

The main cause is processed fructose which is often added to sweeten up sodas, juices, sauces, desserts and even so-called "healthy" meals and drinks. Even kids are consuming more sugar these days, setting them up for a era of poor health and nutrition.

Changing up the fats we eat has caused a problem, too. For years, many have been made to believe that animal fats, coconut oil and other healthy saturated fats could cause heart problems. People exchanged them for processed vegetable oils like canola and corn oils that can actually cause hormonal differences and metabolic changes within your body.

Over the years, repeated use of these oils has helped perpetuate the obesity problem, and more and more people have shied away from the important, healthy and naturally-occurring fats we once used.

Moreover, the increased ingesting of vegetable and processed oils have flooded our bodies with omega-6 fats throwing off the delicate balance of fatty acids. When fatty acids aren't properly balanced, it can lead to heart disease, depression Alzheimer's, arthritis, diabetes and, in some people, even certain types of cancer. Omega-3s (the fats that come from fish and fish oil) and omega-6s need to be in balance.

That means 1 serving of one, for every 1 serving of the other. Today's American eats about twice as many omega-6s as omega-3s.

Accessibility foods have hurt the American health as well. As the speed of our society has quickened, more and more people are eating on the go.

They're picking up fried, fast food and eating it in the car, they're grabbing pre-packaged snacks and drinks at the gas station, and they're eating foods that aren't made fresh or naturally. It's a trend that, while easy, cheap and appropriate, has caused much more hurt than good.

Getting Back to Basics

The real key to getting the modern diet back on track is to get back to basics. Centuries and centuries ago, cavemen didn't have obesity problems. Why? Because they ate from the earth fresh vegetables and fruits, grass-fed meats and other natural, unprocessed and untouched foods.

This diet needs to serve as inspiration for today's society. Fresh produce should be a part of every meal, and instead of avoiding fats, we need to consume plenty of good, healthy fats for our bodies to thrive on.

The so-called "low fat" phase of the 80s and 90s has caused immense damage to our country's health. Fats are vital to our body's function. In fact, for optimal health, about 50 to 80 percent of your daily calories should come from good fats! That means nuts, fish, avocado, seeds, olive oil, coconut oil, eggs and beans all things found in nature.

HISTORY OF INTERMITTENT FASTING

Compared to traditional "dieting," fasting is simple and unambiguous. It's always been done. You already unconsciously do IF whenever you skip breakfast or dinner.

Historically, during hunter gatherer days, our dynasties were in a fasting state while seeking food.

When agriculture was established, civilization came next. But when food was scarce or seasons changed, fasting was still a way of life. Cities and castles stored grain and cured meat for the winter. Before irrigation, lack of rain meant famine, and people fasted to make their stored food last as long as possible until the rains came back and it was possible for crops to survive again.

Religions flourished in this arrangement of people living closer together, distributing and spreading belief and traditions. And religions also prescribed fasting.

Hinduism calls fasting "Vaasa" and observes it during special days or festivals, as a private penance, or to honor their personal gods. Islam and Judaism have Ramadan and Yom Kippur, when it's forbidden to work, eat, drink, wash, wear leather and have intercourse. In Catholicism, it's six weeks of fasting before Easter or before Holy Week.

THE SCIENCE OF INTERMITTENT FASTING

The modern era of agriculture and factory-laden "food" (or food-like substances) has absolutely changed the way humans view and consume food on a daily basis, leading to the laundry list of health problems that our society faces today.

Although IF is an primeval practice, the science after its many health benefits is just recently being exposed to mainstream society.

When you fast, you basically allow your body to naturally cleanse, repair and regenerate itself for optimal function.

Three of the main health-promoting mechanisms associated with fasting include the metabolic regulation of circadian biology, the gut microbiome and different lifestyle behaviors.

Circadian Biology

Humans (and other organisms) have evolved to develop a circadian clock that ensures physiological processes within your body are performed at optimal times throughout the day.

These circadian rhythms occur across 24-hour light-dark cycles and influence changes in biology and behavior.

Interrupting this circadian rhythm negatively impacts metabolism which contributes to obesity and associated diseases such as type 2 diabetes, cardiovascular disease and cancer.

This is where intermittent fasting comes in.

Feeding signals seem to be the main timing cue for how your circadian rhythms function and thus control certain metabolic, physiological and behavioral pathways that contribute to overall health and longevity.

Certain behavioral interventions such as (you guessed it!) intermittent fasting can help synchronize your circadian rhythms leading to improved fluctuations in gene illustration, reprogramming of energy metabolism and improved hormonal and body weight regulation, all factors that play a vital role in optimizing your health outcomes.

The Gut Microbiome

The gastrointestinal (GI) tract, better known as the "gut," plays an extremely important role in regulating several processes within your body.

Many functions of the gut (and nearly every physiological and biochemical function in your body) are influenced by your circadian rhythm described above.

For example, gastric emptying, blood flow and metabolic responses to glucose are greater during the daytime than at night.

So, it's likely that a chronically disturbed circadian rhythm can affect gut function contributing to impaired metabolism and increased risk for chronic disease.

The gut microbiome, also known as our "second brain," has been the subject of extensive research in both health and disease due to its profound involvement in human metabolism, physiology, nutrition and immune function.

Intermittent fasting has a direct and positive influence on the gut microbiome through:

- Reduced gut permeability
- Diminished systemic inflammation
- Promotion of energy balance by enhancing gut integrity.

Research on both the gut and intermittent fasting continues to emerge while the potential for

prevention and treatment of diseases is becoming more widely understood.

Lifestyle Behaviors

Intermittent fasting is shown to help modify different health performances such as caloric intake (i.e. how much you eat), energy expenditure (how much you move) and sleep.

There's no surprise that these three factors contribute to one of the biggest draws to intermittent fasting today: weight loss.

A recent study showed that increasing the nightly fasting duration to greater than 14 hours led to a significant decrease in caloric intake and weight with improvements to:

- Energy levels
- Sleep satisfaction
- Satiety at bedtime

Intermittent fasting also reduces nighttime eating, which contributes to poor sleep quality and reduced sleep duration leading to insulin resistance and increased risk of obesity, diabetes, cardiovascular disease and cancer.

Fasting puts an adaptive cellular stress on the body which in turn allows your body to cope with more severe stressors that may occur and thus protect against potential disease progressions.

This concept is known as hormesis when an exposure to a mild stress causes cells in your body to become more resilient against other, more severe stressors.

Think of it this way – what doesn't kill you really does make you stronger!

BENEFIT OF INTERMITTENT FASTING

The benefits of intermittent fasting are vast. Fasting gets a bad rap, but there is real science behind the technique of fasting, in particular, intermittent fasting. Many people think that someone who is fasting has an eating disorder, but nothing could be farther from the truth.

The truth is that in today's society, we eat far too much and too often. Our bodies are very precise mechanisms that, allowed to run properly, will take care of us far beyond our imagination. The problem lies with the fact that historically, for thousands and thousands of years, we were a species with little food resources and we worked long and hard each and every day for the morsels we did get. Today, we have a plethora of food, most of it very fattening, and sedentary lifestyles. This both contributes to obesity and disease.

Fasting intermittently can eliminate many problems caused from overeating and sitting around all day instead of out hunting and gathering. The fact is that we have not evolved enough to be able to handle all the calories that we ingest on a daily basis, our bodies still operate as if we were hunter and gatherers. Not until the 20th century did most people have food at the ready, so 100 years is not even close to adequate time to adjust how our body operates.

Extreme blood pressure, excessive cholesterol, and obesity are all problems that can be helped with intermittent fasting. A particularly effective fasting plan is called the Fast 5. This plan requires you to fast for 19 hours every day and eat for 5 consecutive hours. It is important to note that you DO eat when fasting intermittently. Eating is essential to your health, but eating once or twice a day during a short period is more natural to our bodies than stuffing them 12 out of 24 hours in a day. Again, up until the 20th century, most people only managed to eat once a day for thousands of years.

The pattern of eating called "Intermittent Fasting" usually means one fasts for a period of time and eats for a period of time. Many choose a

24 hour cycle of fasting, then eat healthy the next day, and continue this process as a lifestyle change.

Research has been done on animals to find the benefits of this type of fasting, and you will be happy to know it really can be beneficial to your health!

Intermittent fasting can add 40%-56% more years to your life! That in itself is reason enough to do it. However other benefits include body weight reduction and fat oxidation.

When you fast your body is forced to scavenge for fuel thus removing aged and damaged cells in the process. This sort of cleanses the body of unwanted and unwanted things and helps the weight loss and benefits of the good food choices be increased and more beneficial to your body.

Rats have been shown to have long-term and improved survival after heart failure after being on an IF eating plan, too. Researchers are also saying that it might help age related deficits in cognitive function, too, so that tells me that it might help ward off Alzheimer's Disease and other types of Dementia!

Your risk of heart disease and other heart ailments may also be decreased when you start a healthy intermittent fasting regimen. Your risk for other chronic illnesses and diseases will also most likely be reduced.

A improved you can begin with intermittent fasting and healthy food choices! Keep carbs to 50-100 grams per day. Many women eat between 1200-1500 calories per day, and when limiting their carbs, they are still losing weight. Men can handle up to 2000 calories per day. Of course less is best, and you need to determine caloric intake based on your activity such as working hard and exercising.

Drink lots of fluids, especially water and exercise in the evenings if possible. This will help with those late night cravings.

Once you start eating and drinking healthier, your body won't crave as much (if any) junk food, so making healthy food choices will simply get easier and easier as you progress in the intermittent fasting routine.

Alternate Day Fasting or ADF means alternating days of eating and not eating any food, but there is also an intermittent fasting called Modified Fasting where you consume about 20% of your normal calories one day and then eat normally (but healthy) the next day. This is frequently more attainable for people because they feel less deprived when they are able to at least eat something daily, and it still has most of the benefits of the ADF regimen.

Whatever you choose to do, make sure you tell your health care professional of your plans so he or she is aware and can work with you to reach your goals. If you want to lose weight, lose fat and feel better, then intermittent fasting might be the answer for you!

The fasting periods were often called 'cleanses', 'detoxifications', or 'purifications', but the idea is similar – e.g. to abstain from eating food for a certain period of time, often for health reasons. People imagined that this period of abstinence from food would clear their bodies' systems of toxins and rejuvenate them. They may have been more correct than they knew.

Some of the purported health benefits of intermittent fasting include:

- Weight and body fat loss
- Increased fat burning
- Lowered blood insulin and sugar levels
- Possibly reversal of type 2 diabetes
- Possibly improved mental clarity and concentration
- Possibly increased energy
- Possibly increased growth hormone, at least in the short term
- Possibly an improved blood cholesterol profile
- Possibly a reduction in the risk of Alzheimer's disease
- Possibly longer life
- Possibly activation of cellular cleansing by stimulating autophagy
- Possibly reduction of inflammation.

Fasting offers many important unique advantages that are not available in typical diets.

Where diets can complicate life, intermittent fasting may simplify it. Where diets can be expensive, intermittent fasting can be free. Where diets can take time, fasting saves time. Where diets may be limited in their availability, fasting is available anywhere. And as discussed earlier, fasting is a potentially powerful method for lowering insulin and decreasing body weight.

FASTING AND AUTOPHAGY

But what is autophagy? The word derives from the Greek auto (self) and phage in (to eat). So the word literally means to eat oneself. Essentially, this is the body's mechanism of getting rid of all the broken down, old cell machinery (organelles, proteins and cell membranes) when there's no longer enough energy to sustain it. It is a regulated, orderly process to degrade and recycle cellular components.

There is a related, better known process called apoptosis also known as programmed cell death. Cells, after a certain number of division, are programmed to die. While this may sound kind of macabre at first, realize that this process is crucial in maintaining good health. For example, suppose you own a car. You love this car. You have great memories in it. You love to ride it.

But after a few years, it starts to look kind of beat up. After a few more, it's not looking so great. The car is costing you thousands of dollars every year to maintain. It's breaking down all the time. Is it better to keep it around when it's nothing but a hunk of junk? Apparently not. So you get rid of it and buy a snazzy new car.

The same thing happens in the body. Cells become old and junky. It is better that they be programmed to die when their useful life is done. It sounds really cruel, but that's life. That's the process of apoptosis, where cells are pre-destined to die after a certain amount of time. It's like leasing a car. After a certain amount of time, you get rid of the car, whether it's still working or not. Then you get a new car. You don't have to worry about it breaking down at the worst possible time.

Autophagy – replacing old parts of the cell

The same process also happens at a sub-cellular level. You don't necessarily need to replace the entire car. Sometimes, you just need to replace the battery, throw out the old one and get a new one. This also happens in the cells. Instead of killing off the entire cell (apoptosis), you only want to replace some cell parts. That is the process of autophagy, where sub-cellular organelles are destroyed and new ones are rebuilt to replace it.

Old cell membranes, organelles and other cellular debris can be removed. This is done by sending it to the lysosome which is a specialized organelle containing enzymes to degrade proteins.

What activates autophagy?

Nutrient deprivation is the key activator of autophagy. Remember that glucagon is kind of the opposite hormone to insulin. It's like the game we played as kids 'opposite day'. If insulin goes up, glucagon goes down.

If insulin goes down, glucagon goes up. As we eat, insulin goes up and glucagon goes down. When we don't eat (fast) insulin goes down and glucagon goes up. This increase in glucagon stimulates the process of autophagy. In fact, fasting (raises glucagon) provides the greatest known boost to autophagy.

This is in essence a form of cellular cleansing. The body identifies old and substandard cellular equipment and marks it for destruction. It is the accumulation of all this junk that may be responsible for many of the effects of aging.

Fasting is actually far more beneficial than just stimulating autophagy. It does two good things. By stimulating autophagy, we are clearing out all our old, junky proteins and cellular parts. At the same time, fasting also stimulates growth hormone, which tells our body to start producing some new snazzy parts for the body. We are really giving our bodies the complete renovation.

You need to get rid of the old stuff before you can put in new stuff. Think about renovating your kitchen. If you have old, crappy 1970s style lime green cabinets sitting around, you need to junk them before putting in some new ones. So the process of destruction (removal) is just as important as the process of creation. If you simply tried to put in new cabinets without taking out the old ones, it would be pretty ugly. So fasting may in some ways reverse the aging process, by getting rid of old cellular junk and replacing it with new parts.

A highly controlled process

Autophagy is a highly regulated process. If it runs amok, out of control, this would be detrimental, so it must be carefully controlled. In mammalian cells, total depletion of amino acids is a strong signal for autophagy, but the role of individual amino acids is more variable. However, the plasma amino acid levels vary only a little. Amino acid signals and growth factor / insulin signals are thought to converge on the mTOR pathway sometimes called the master regulator of nutrient signaling.

So, during autophagy, old junky cell components are broken down into the component amino acids (the building block of proteins). What happens to these amino acids? In the early stages of starvation, amino acid levels start to increase. It is thought that these amino acids derived from autophagy are delivered to the liver for gluconeogenesis.

They can also be broken down into glucose through the tricarboxylic acid (TCA) cycle. The third potential fate of amino acids is to be incorporated into new proteins.

The consequences of accumulating old junky proteins all over the place can be seen in two main conditions Alzheimer's Disease (AD) and cancer.

Alzheimer's Disease involves the accumulation of abnormal protein either amyloid beta or Tau protein which gums up the brain system. It would make sense that a process like autophagy that has the ability to clear out old protein could prevent the development of AD.

What turns off autophagy? Eating. Glucose, insulin (or decreased glucagon) and proteins all turn off this self-cleaning process. And it doesn't take much. Even a small amount of amino acid (leucine) could stop autophagy cold. So this process of autophagy is unique to fasting something not found in simple caloric restriction or dieting.

There is a balance here, of course. You get sick from too much autophagy as well as too little. Which gets us back to the natural cycle of life feast and fast. Not constant dieting. This allows for cell growth during eating, and cellular cleansing during fasting balance. Life is all about balance.

CHAPTER 2 :

TYPES OF INTERMITTENT FASTING

WHOLE DAY FASTING

When it comes to eating programs, humans are built for suppleness. It's a complete myth that people "need" to eat three times a day (or 6 meals a day, or on any other specific schedule). Think about that for a minute: there's no way we would have survived the caveman days if we needed to eat every few hours. If we were really that fragile, we would have died off ages ago. 3 meals a day is the typical cultural pattern, but who says your particular body might not do better on some other eating schedule? Some people prefer to eat every day, but within a restricted window. Other people eat normally most of the time, but occasionally embark on long fasts.

But there's also an option in between: eat normally on some days, but then periodically go on a 24-hour fast. A common option is alternate-day fasting, but some people also do 1-3 fast days per week on set days.

The Case for One-Day Fasts

For weight loss, the idea of occasional 24-hour fasts is basically low-effort calorie reduction. Sure, most people will be hungrier and eat more on the day after their fast, but they probably won't eat twice as much as they otherwise would. And that calorie reduction comes without the need to count the calories in anything you eat the only question is yes or no on food for the day.

This is more or less the same idea as a limited eating window (say, eating only between noon and 8pm). But some people find that cramming all their food into a short eating window gives them an upset stomach for those people, one-day fasting might be easier because on "feeding" days, you can spread out your meals normally.

In terms of benefits that aren't related to weight loss, fasting has been claimed to help with everything from cancer prevention to life extension, but most of those claims are based on animal studies, and it's not clear whether the benefits in humans live up to the hype.

In this post, we'll take a look at studies on one-day fasts and alternate-day fasting, focusing on some specific questions:

• Do regular fast days' work for weight loss?

• Do regular fast days have benefits other than weight loss?

• Are the effects different in lean vs. obese subjects?

At the end, we'll also take a look at variations on the one-day fast theme, including modified fasting.

One-Day Fasts: The Big Picture

A lot of the research on this has focused precisely on alternate-day fasting (eat on Day 1, fast on Day 2, eat on Day 3, fast on Day 4, etc.). In terms of weight loss, here's a big-picture overview of review studies:

- Alternate-day fasting is just as effective as very-low calorie diets for weight loss, but it may be easier: some patients found it simpler to fast every day than to restrict calories every day.
- Unfortunately, an alternate-day fasting scheme doesn't prevent your metabolism from fighting back against weight loss. This review looked exclusively at metabolic adaptations to weight loss. You might expect that alternate-day fasting would be superior to constant dieting here, but the study didn't actually find evidence of that – both were about the same.
    As for non-weight-related benefits, the evidence in humans is mixed but encouraging:
- A 2007 review of alternate-day fasting found that it may help to improve blood lipids (higher HDL cholesterol, lower triglycerides), but also found that alternate-day fasting and ordinary calorie limitation were equally good for insulin levels and blood sugar control.

- Another study found that severe calorie restriction (less than 20% of energy needs) on alternate days reduced inflammation and oxidative stress in overweight adults with asthma.
- Finally, this study found that intermittent energy restriction (less than 25% of energy needs) reduced inflammation and improved blood lipids in overweight women.

Is it a magical cancer stoppage/cure tactic? No, but nothing really is. In overweight subjects, one-day fasts seem to reduce some measures of overall physical stress and chronic poor health.

Obese vs. Non-Obese Subjects

Some more dramatic weight-loss approaches (e.g. protein-sparing modified fasts) are fine for people with a lot of weight to lose, but don't work so well for the last 5-10 pounds. So what about occasional one-day fasts?

This analysis looked at alternate-day fasting in 16 non-obese subjects (8 men, 8 women). The subjects fasted every other day for 22 days. On average, they lost about 2.5% of their initial body weight (so a 150-pound person would lose just under 4 pounds). But they never stopped being hungry on fasting days.

Reflecting that most people don't want to be hungry every other day for the rest of their lives, this suggests that alternate-day fasting might not be the best strategy for people who are already fairly close to their target weight.

On the other hand, not everyone responds the same way. Some fairly lean people might be perfectly happy taking regular fast days. The study did show that it worked fine, just that it wasn't pleasant. If you don't notice the same amount of hunger, it might be just the thing for you.

Variations on a Theme

Most of the studies so far have been in alternate-day fasting. But the same ideas (a hormonal break from digestion, low-effort calorie reduction) still apply to vaguely less rigorous fasting proprieties like...

Fasting 1-3 days per week

The benefit: makes your social calendar easier.

One big barrier to alternate-day fasting is that most of us have a weekly schedule, and weeks have an odd number of days. Fasting every other day means that you're frequently changing the day of the week when your fast happens, which can be inconvenient. It may be easier for some people to fast on specific calendar days, rather than every other day.

Is it Worth a Try?

Probably yes if...

- You're primarily interested in weight loss, especially if you have quite a bit of weight to lose
- You don't mind the idea of going a whole day with no or very little food
- You have a lot of weight to lose.
    Probably no if...
- You'd rather just eat less every day (there's no evidence that alternate-day fasting works better, so you may as well do what you prefer).
- You do very intense exercise most days or every day.
- You get unpleasant side effects (weakness, dizziness, feeling cold, etc.) from fasting. If you still want to fast in this case, you might consider the classic "intermittent fasting" design with a compressed eating window, which can be a little less intense but still has similar benefits.

Have you ever tried daily fasts? How many times a week? Did you fully fast, or did you do a modified fast?

5:2 INTERMITTENT FASTING

Intermittent fasting is an eating pattern that involves regular fasting.

The 5:2 diet, also known as The Fast Diet, is currently the most popular intermittent fasting diet.

It was popularized by British journalist Michael Mosley.

It's called the 5:2 diet because five days of the week are normal eating days, while the other two restrict calories to 500–600 per day.

Because there are no requests about which foods to eat but rather when you should eat them, this diet is more of a regime.

Many people find this way of eating to be simpler to stick to than a traditional calorie-restricted diet.

This level explains everything you need to know about the 5:2 diet.

What is the 5:2 diet?

The 5:2 diet gets its name because it involves eating regularly for 5 days of the week while drastically curbing caloric intake on the other 2 two days.

While the 5:2 diet is a popular form of intermittent fasting, the term fasting is slightly misleading.

Distinct a true fast, which involves eating nothing for a set extent of time, the goal of the 5:2 diet is to cut caloric intake on fasting days to 25 percent or just one-quarter of a person's regular intake on the remaining days.

For example, a person who regularly eats about 2,000 calories per day would eat 500 calories on fasting days.

Importantly, fasting days are not successive because it is vital to give the body the calories and nutrients it needs to thrive.

People typically space their fasting days out, for example, by taking their reduced-calorie days on Monday and Thursday or Wednesday and Saturday.

Part of the diet's appeal is this flexibility. Instead of severely restricting the foods a person can eat, the 5:2 diet focuses on strict caloric limitation on only 2 days of the week.

This may help some people feel more gratified with their diet, as they will not feel that they are missing out all the time.

The 5 normal days of the 5:2 diet should still involve a nourishing diet, however. Loading up on sugary or processed foods for 5 days and then having a small break may not be as helpful as keeping a trend of clean eating during the entire week.

What are the benefits?

The 5:2 diet can have several benefits, including:

Weight loss

For the most part, people who follow the 5:2 diet plan are looking to lose weight.

To lose weight, a person typically needs to eat fewer calories than they burn. Nutritionists call this a caloric deficit.

When someone follows this correctly, the 5:2 diet may be a simple, straightforward way to cut calories, which may help burn extra fat.

While there are not many studies on the 5:2 diet specially, initial studies on intermittent fasting seem promising.

A review in the Annual Review of Nourishment noted that in animal studies, a related intermittent fasting diet led to a cutback in fat tissue and the cells that store fat.

A 2018 review and meta-analysis compared intermittent fasting to simple calorie curb diets. This research noted that intermittent fasting is as effective as calorie restriction when it comes to weight loss and successful metabolic health.

Reducing the risk of type 2 diabetes

Original studies also suggest an intermittent calorie diet may also help shrink the risk of diabetes in some people.

Research from 2014 suggests that both intermittent fasting diets and calorie restriction diets helped reduce fasting insulin levels and insulin resistance in adults who were overweight or obese. The reviewers did call for more research to confirm these findings.

This does not suggest that intermittent fasting is a better diet, just an equally effective alternative for people who find calorie restriction diets difficult.

The 5:2 Diet for Weight Loss

If you need to lose weight, the 5:2 diet can be very effective when done right.

This is mainly because the 5:2 eating pattern helps you consume fewer calories.

Therefore, it is very important not to compensate for the fasting days by eating much more on the non-fasting days.

Intermittent fasting does not cause more weight loss than regular calorie restriction if total calories are matched.

That said, fasting protocols similar to the 5:2 diet have shown a lot of promise in weight loss studies:

- A recent review found that modified alternate-day fasting led to weight loss of 3–8% over the course of 3–24 weeks.
- In the same study, participants lost 4–7% of their waist circumference, meaning that they lost a lot of harmful belly fat.
- Intermittent fasting causes a much smaller reduction in muscle mass when compared to weight loss with conventional calorie restriction.

Intermittent fasting is even more effective when combined with exercise, such as endurance or strength training.

What to Do If You Feel Unwell or Uncontrollably Hungry

During the first few fast days, you can expect to have episodes of tremendous hunger. It is also normal to feel a little weaker or slower than usual.

However, you'll be surprised at how quickly the hunger fades, especially if you try to keep busy with work or other errands.

Additionally, most people find that the fast days become easier after the first few fasts.

If you are not used to fasting, it may be a good idea to keep a small snack handy during your first few fasts, just in case you feel faint or ill.

But if you repeatedly find yourself feeling ill or faint during fast days, have something to eat and talk with your doctor about whether you should continue.

Intermittent fasting is not for everyone, and some people are unable to tolerate it.

Is the 5:2 safe for everyone?

The 5:2 diet may be a helpful substitute to some people looking for a less restrictive diet plan, but it is not for everyone.

People who are prone to low blood sugar or easily feel dizzy or fatigued if they do not eat may not want to follow a diet that involves fasting.

Pregnant or breastfeeding women must also avoid fasting. Children and teenagers should avoid fasting unless under the direct guidance of a doctor, as their bodies are still emerging.

Anyone with a chronic condition, such as diabetes, can consult a doctor before trying any diet that includes fasting.

Who Should Avoid the 5:2 Diet, or Intermittent Fasting Overall?

Although intermittent fasting is very safe for healthy, well-nourished people, it does not suit everyone.

Some people should avoid dietary restrictions and fasting completely. These include:

- Individuals with a history of eating disorders.
- Individuals who often experience drops in blood sugar levels.

- Pregnant women, nursing mothers, teenagers, children and individuals with type 1 diabetes.
- People who are malnourished, underweight or have known nutrient deficiencies.
- Women who are trying to conceive or have fertility issues.

Furthermore, intermittent fasting may not be as beneficial for some women as it is for men.

Some women have reported that their menstrual period stopped while they were following this type of eating pattern. However, things went back to normal when they returned to a regular diet.

Therefore, women should be careful when starting any form of intermittent fasting, and stop doing it instantly if any adverse effects occur.

The 5:2 diet is an easy, effective way to lose weight and improve metabolic health.

Many people find it much easier to stick to than a conventional calorie-restricted diet.

If you're looking to lose weight or improve your health, the 5:2 diet is definitely something to consider.

TIME RESTRICTED FASTING

Time-restricted eating is a type of diet that focuses on the timing of eating. Instead of controlling the types of food or number of calories that people consume, this diet restricts the amount of time they can spend eating.

A person on a time-restricted eating diet will only eat during specific hours of the day. Outside of this period, they will fast.

In this book, we look at what time-restricted eating is, whether or not it works, and what effect it has on muscle gain. We also provide beginner's tips on how to get started with this diet plan.

What is time-restricted eating?

Time-restricted eating means that a person eats all of their meals and snacks within a particular window of time each day. This timeframe can vary according to the person's preference and the plan they choose to follow.

Typically, though, the eating window in time-restricted programs ranges from 6–12 hours a day.

Outside of this period, a person consumes no calories. They should, however, drink water or no-calorie beverages to remain hydrated. In some time-restricted diet plans, people may also consume unsweetened coffee or tea with no cream.

Time-restricted eating is a type of intermittent fasting. Intermittent fasting refers to any diet that alternates between periods of restricting calories and eating normally.

Although time-restricted eating will not work for everyone, those who have their doctor's approval may find it beneficial. Some recent studies have shown that it can aid weight loss and may lower the risk of metabolic diseases, such as diabetes.

Time-restricted eating can help a person to restrict their food intake without having to count calories. It may also be a healthy way to avoid common diet pitfalls, such as late-night snacking. However, people with diabetes or other health issues should speak to their doctor before trying this type of diet.

Health Effects of Time-Restricted Eating

Time-restricted eating may have several health benefits, including weight loss, better heart health and lower blood sugar levels.

Weight Loss.

Several studies of both normal-weight and overweight people restricted eating to a window of 7–12 hours, reporting weight loss of up to 5% over 2–4 weeks.

However, other studies in normal-weight people have reported no weight loss with eating windows of similar duration.

Whether or not you will experience weight loss with time-restricted eating probably depends on whether or not you manage to eat fewer calories within the eating period.

If this flair of eating helps you eat little calories each day, it can produce weight loss over time.

If this is not the case for you, time-restricted eating may not be your best bet for weight loss.

Heart Health.

Several substances in your blood can affect your risk of heart disease, and one of these important substances is cholesterol.

"Bad" LDL cholesterol increases your risk of heart disease, while "good" HDL cholesterol decreases your risk.

One study found that four weeks of time-restricted eating during an 8-hour window lowered "bad" LDL cholesterol by over 10% in both men and women.

However, other study using a similar length of eating window did not show any benefits on cholesterol levels.

Both studies used normal-weight adults, so the inconsistent results may be due to disparities in weight loss.

When participants lost weight with time-restricted eating, their cholesterol improved. When they did not lose weight, it did not improve.

Several studies have shown that slightly longer eating windows of 10–12 hours may also improve cholesterol.

In these studies, "bad" LDL cholesterol was reduced by up to 10–35% over four weeks in normal-weight people.

Blood Sugar.

The amount of glucose, or "sugar," in your blood is important for your health. Having too much sugar in your blood can lead to diabetes and damage several parts of your body.

Overall, the effects of time-restricted eating on blood sugar are not entirely clear.

Several studies in normal-weight people have reported decreases in blood sugar of up to 30%, while a different report showed a 20% increase in blood sugar.

More research is needed to decide if time-restricted eating can improve blood sugar.

Does time-restricted eating work?

No single diet plan will work for everyone. While some people are likely to have achievement with time-restricted eating, others may not benefit from it. It is best to speak to a doctor before trying time-restricted eating, or any other diet.

Many of the studies on time-restricted eating have been small or have involved animals rather than people, so large human studies are still necessary.

Nonetheless, some recent research shows that time-restricted eating may have the potential to lead to weight loss and health upgrading:

- In a report designed to mimic obesity in postmenopausal women, mice on a time-restricted feeding plan lost weight and saw health improvements, unlike the mice that ate around the clock.
- Another study found that mice that only ate within an 8–9 hour period each day lost weight and had improved metabolic fitness.
- In one study, investigators allowed obese rats to eat for only 9 hours a day over the 5 weekdays. The young adult rats whose eating was time-restricted gained less weight than those that ate at any time. However, weight gain was the same in both groups of older adult rats.

- A small study found that time-restricted eating helped people with obesity to lower their calorie consumption and lose a small amount of weight. The study limited eating to an 8-hour period and lasted for 12 weeks.

Although these studies suggest that time-restricted eating has potential, not all research shows a benefit.

A 2017 review concluded that intermittent calorie restriction, including time-restricted feeding, offers no major advantage over warning calorie intake each day.

Gaining muscle and time-restricted eating

Exploration has shown that time-restricted eating can work well alongside efforts to build muscle.

One study investigated time-restricted eating in young men who followed a set resistance training program for 8 weeks. The men restricted their eating window to 4 hours on the 4 non-workout days each week.

The authors concluded that participants who followed the time-restricted eating plan reduced their calorie intake without losing strength. However, time-restricted eating did not result in reductions in body weight or body fat compared to a standard diet.

Another study placed resistance-trained men into either a time-restricted eating group or a normal diet group. Those in the time-restricted eating group ate 100 percent of their calorie needs during an 8-hour window each day for 8 weeks. The time-restricted eating led to a decrease in body fat with no reduction in muscle mass.

Time-Restricted Eating Plus Exercise

If you exercise regularly, you may wonder how time-restricted eating will affect your workouts.

One eight-week study examined time-restricted eating in young men who followed a weight-training program.

It found that the men performing time-restricted eating were able to increase their strength just as much as the control group that ate normally.

A similar study in adult men who weight trained compared time-restricted eating during an 8-hour eating window to a normal eating pattern.

It found that the men eating all of their calories in an 8-hour period each day lost about 15% of their body fat, while the control group did not lose any body fat.

What's more, both groups had similar advances in strength and endurance.

Based on these studies, it appears that you can exercise and make good progress while following a time-restricted eating program.

However, research is needed in women and those performing an aerobic exercise like running or swimming.

Beginner's guide to time-restricted eating

One of the main advantages of time-restricted eating is that it requires no special food or equipment. After getting a doctor's approval, a person can begin a time-restricted eating plan immediately.

However, as with any diet, some thought and planning can increase the likelihood of success. The following tips can help to make time-restricted eating safer and more effective:

Starting gradually

Start with a shorter fasting period and then gradually increase it over time. For example, start with a fasting period of 10:00 p.m. to 6:30 a.m. Then increase this by 30 minutes every 3 days to reach the desired fasting period.

Studies have suggested that restricting feeding periods to less than 6 hours is unlikely to offer extra advantages over more extended feeding stages.

Exercising without overdoing it

It is tempting to start a vigorous exercise plan alongside a diet for faster results. However, with time-restricted eating, this could make the fasting period more difficult.

People may wish to keep their existing exercise program the same until their body adjusts to the new eating plan. This can help to avoid increased hunger from extra workouts, which could cause diet burnout or failure.

Focusing on protein and fiber

Hunger can be difficult for people who do not have experience of fasting for several hours each day. Choosing foods rich in fiber and protein during the eating window can help to combat this. These nutrients help a person feel full and can prevent a blood sugar crash or food cravings.

For example, eat whole-grain bread and pasta rather than white or refined grains. Choose a snack which includes protein in the form of lean meat, egg, tofu, or nuts.

Avoiding worrying about setbacks

It is normal to have days where time-restricted eating does not work out. For example, a night out with friends, a special occasion, or a diet slip-up may lead to people eating outside of their fixed eating window.

However, this does not mean that they should quit. It is best to see setbacks as an opportunity to get back on track. The next day, people can recommence the time-restricted eating plan and continue toward their goal.

16 8 INTERMITTENT FASTING

The problem with this popular method is that you're not making decisions based on how full or hungry you feel, but rather on a restricted time window a setup that can flop in the long run. Here's what you need to know about 16:8 fasting before you start missing meals.

What is the 16:8 diet?

The 16:8 diet is a type of time-restricted fasting done to achieve better health or lose weight.

On the 16:8 diet, you spend 16 hours of each day consuming nothing but unsweetened beverages like water, coffee, and tea. The remaining eight-hour window is when you eat all of your meals and snacks. Most people do this by starting a fast at night, skipping breakfast, and eating their first meal in the middle of the day. No foods are inherently off limits during that time, but some people will follow the keto diet to supercharge their weight loss.

While the term intermittent fasting (or IF) may be new to many of us, the practice isn't all that different from the way our sassociates likely lived: Hunt, gather, and eat during daylight; sleep and fast during darkness.

Is 16:8 fasting good for weight loss?

Some studies have found that there's virtually no difference between people who regularly practiced intermittent fasting and those who simply cut back their calorie intake overall.

A growing body of research demonstrates that a better scheme is optimizing nutritious quality of what you eat (veggies, fruit, lean protein, whole grains, and healthy fats) versus fasting or counting calories.

Also, science suggests any potential benefit from fasting is quickly undone during the eating part of the cycle, in which appetite-suppressing hormones switch gears to make you feel even hungrier than you felt at baseline.

Is fasting 16 hours a day healthy?

Forms of intermittent fasting like the 16:8 diet rely on the concept that fasting cuts oxidative stress on the body, which can decrease inflammation and the risk of chronic diseases.

It's also theorized that fasting gives your vital organs, digestive and absorptive hormones, and metabolic functions a "break," though that's mostly unfounded in humans. Since our bodies secrete insulin to help our cells absorb sugar, fasting is linked to reducing our susceptibility to insulin conflict over time. (High insulin levels ultimately put us at risk for a whole host of diseases).

However, research has also linked fasting to increases in LDL cholesterol (the "bad" kind). Intermittent fasting can make you feel dizzy and nauseated and cause periods of low-blood sugar and dehydration.

Despite the fact that most 16:8 enthusiasts drink water during fasting periods, it may not be enough (reminder: food itself provides quite a bit of water).

I also have a much deeper concern about the messy eating behaviors that may arise from intermittent fasting. Research shows that fasting for a period of time followed by a limited window for eating primes you to overeat. It's a cycle that can be difficult to get out of because it impairs our body's natural hunger cues and metabolism. Regulated eating may also lead to an increased hazard of misery and anxiety.

This is particularly concerning for women, who have historically been more likely to develop eating disorders. The allotted periods of restriction followed by eating lends itself to binge-purge tendencies that cannot (and should not) be ignored. According to the National Eating Disorders Association, periods of fasting and binging are considered risk factors for eating disorders.

Should you try 16:8 fasting?

Eventually, it's a personal choice. But there are a few beneficial behaviors you can try without committing to the dodgier elements of 16-hour fasts. The first is to better comprehend mindfulness and how it relates to your food choices. To get started, consider these questions when you're deciding when and what to eat:

Where are you physically when you decide to eat?

Many of us eat based on scenario, not hunger levels. Case in point: Raise your hand if you've ever gone to the movies after dinner and suddenly wanted popcorn? Yep, me too!

By considering the moments when you eat, you may become aware of patterns you didn't notice before. Say you're a person who loves to graze during The Bachelor. If you're fasting after 8 p.m., you've automatically cut hours and subsequently, calories from your post-dinner snacking.

Are you getting enough sleep?

If you've cut out late-night snacking, that alone could help you go to bed earlier a very crucial component to any weight loss plan. Getting seven hours of sleep per night as been linked to better weight management, reduced risk of chronic disease, and improved metabolism.

HOW TO START FASTING

Despite its recent surge in popularity, fasting is a practice that dates back centuries and plays a central role in many cultures and religions.

Defined as the self-denial from all or some foods or drinks for a set period of time, there are many different ways of fasting.

In general, most types of fasts are performed over 24–72 hours.

Intermittent fasting, on the other hand, involves cycling between periods of eating and fasting, ranging from a few hours to a few days at a time.

FASTING FOR GENERAL HEALTH

Fasting has been shown to have many health benefits, from increased weight loss to better brain function.

1. Promotes Blood Sugar Control by Reducing Insulin Resistance

Several studies have found that fasting may improve blood sugar control, which could be especially useful for those at risk of diabetes.

In fact, one study in 10 people with type 2 diabetes showed that short-term intermittent fasting notably decreased blood sugar levels.

Meanwhile, another review found that both intermittent fasting and alternate-day fasting were as effective as limiting calorie intake at reducing insulin resistance.

Decreasing insulin resistance can increase your body's sensitivity to insulin, allowing it to transport glucose from your bloodstream to your cells more efficiently.

Coupled with the potential blood sugar-lowering effects of fasting, this could help keep your blood sugar steady, preventing spikes and crashes in your blood sugar levels.

Keep in mind though that some studies have found that fasting may impact blood sugar levels differently for men and women.

For example, one small, three-week study showed that practicing alternate-day fasting impaired blood sugar control in women but had no effect in men.

2. Promotes Better Health by Fighting Inflammation

While acute inflammation is a normal immune process used to help fight off infections, chronic inflammation can have serious consequences for your health.

Research shows that inflammation may be involved in the development of chronic conditions, such as heart disease, cancer and rheumatoid arthritis.

Some studies have found that fasting can help decrease levels of inflammation and help promote better health.

One study in 50 healthy adults showed that intermittent fasting for one month significantly decreased levels of inflammatory markers.

Another small study discovered the same effect when people fasted for 12 hours a day for one month.

What's more, one animal study found that following a very low-calorie diet to mimic the effects of fasting reduced levels of inflammation and was positive in the treatment of multiple sclerosis, a chronic inflammatory condition.

3. May Enhance Heart Health by Improving Blood Pressure, Triglycerides and Cholesterol Levels

Heart disease is considered the leading cause of death around the world, accounting for an estimated 31.5% of deaths globally.

Switching up your diet and lifestyle is one of the most effective ways to diminish your risk of heart disease.

Some research has found that incorporating fasting into your repetitive may be especially beneficial when it comes to heart health.

One small study revealed that eight weeks of alternate-day fasting reduced levels of "bad" LDL cholesterol and blood triglycerides by 25% and 32% respectively.

Another study in 110 obese adults showed that fasting for three weeks under medical supervision significantly decreased blood pressure, as well as levels of blood triglycerides, total cholesterol and "bad" LDL cholesterol.

In addition, one study in 4,629 people associated fasting with a lower risk of coronary artery disease, as well as a significantly lower risk of diabetes, which is a major risk factor for heart disease.

4. May Boost Brain Function and Prevent Neurodegenerative Disorders

Though study is mostly limited to animal research, several studies have found that fasting could have a powerful effect on brain health.

One study in mice showed that practicing intermittent fasting for 11 months improved both brain function and brain arrangement.

Other animal studies have reported that fasting could protect brain health and increase the generation of nerve cells to help enhance cognitive function.

Because fasting may also help relieve inflammation, it could also aid in preventing neurodegenerative disorders.

In particular, studies in animals suggest that fasting may protect against and improve outcomes for conditions such as Alzheimer's disease and Parkinson's.

However, more studies are needed to evaluate the effects of fasting on brain function in humans.

5. Aids Weight Loss by Limiting Calorie Intake and Boosting Metabolism

Many dieters pick up fasting looking for a quick and easy way to drop a few pounds.

Theoretically, abstaining from all or certain foods and beverages should decrease your overall calorie intake, which could lead to increased weight loss over time.

Some research has also found that short-term fasting may boost metabolism by increasing levels of the neurotransmitter norepinephrine, which could enhance weight loss.

In fact, one review showed that whole-day fasting could reduce body weight by up to 9% and significantly decrease body fat over 12–24 weeks.

Another analysis found that intermittent fasting over 3–12 weeks was as effective in inducing weight loss as continuous calorie restriction and decreased body weight and fat mass by up to 8% and 16% respectively.

In addition, fasting was found to be more effective than calorie restriction at increasing fat loss while simultaneously preserving muscle tissue.

FASTING FOR WEIGHT LOSS

There are new weight loss plans coming out every day from all around the world. With so many of these new diets and ideas, how can we be sure of which one's work and which ones do not? We simply cannot, and that is the case with the idea of fasting for weight loss. Hearing this now may sound silly, but we should definitely be questioning fasting as an effective means of weight loss because it seems reasonable.

We know that in order to lose weight, you have to be at some sort of calorie deficit. It is simple as that. You will lose weight if you consume less than your use. So with this principle, we would think that fasting would be a great means of dieting because you will be at a great calorie deficit while still having the same calorie use assuming you continue doing the same activities every day.

The truth is, fasting can be effective to some notch or another. It all depends how far you are really taking this process. If you are going to the point of starvation, then fasting will not work. It will simply put too much strain on your body, and it will begin to shut down. As it is shutting down, it goes into fat storing mode.

This means that most anything that you eat from that point forward, if not used immediately, will be converted into fat. This fat will then be stored where ever the body feels is the most fitting.

If by fasting you mean cutting your caloric intake abstemiously, then the fasting for weight loss diet will work for you. Assuming that you still have two to three small meals a day with adequate fluid intake, you would be losing weight in no time.

Because your body will burn around 2000 calories a day normally, this diet will have you burning twice as many calories as you consume. Over the course of a week, this will help you cuts as much as two pounds alone.

You can even add additionally to what you may already be burning through fasting for weight loss. You can take part in other diets such as the fruit juice diet. What is can do is cleanse your system and help clean out some of the excess water that your system is storing for no reason.

You can also add exercise to your calorie deficit to explode your weight loss. Just make sure to get the major food groups and vitamins and minerals every day!

"Fasting for weight loss", is probably the most ignored method of losing weight, yet it has been proven to be a very successful substitute.

When most persons think about the whole idea of "fasting weight loss", they tend to shy away because they view it as too torturous and inhumane; while others view fasting as a fanatical practice only done by highly spiritual gurus.

"Effects of fasting" - what happens in your body when you fast?

When you fast, you abstain from food by drinking purely water (water fast) or natural fruit juice (juice fast), in order to allow the body to initiate its natural healing/cleansing mechanism, which is detoxification. Detoxification is a process by which the body eliminates or deactivates toxins form the colon, liver, kidney, lungs, lymph glands and skin.

When food is no longer entering the body, the body turns to fat reserves for energy, these fat reserves were created when excess glucose and carbohydrates were not used for energy or growth, or excreted, so are therefore converted into fat. When these fat reserves are used for energy during a fast, it releases chemicals (toxins) which are then evicted through the above mentioned organs.

Though fasting detoxifies the body, it's also recommended that a "parasite cleanse" is done to have exact detoxification result.

Fasting - and not starvation

Another reason why people shy away from using fasting as a means to attain weight loss, they think it will make them starve to death or harm them in some other way.

The truth is, only improper fasting leads to starvation or cause other complications. Fasting is only harmful when done without liquid intake or if persistent after hunger returns - when on a total fast. Hunger returning is an indication that all the fat reserves have been used up; usually occurs on a total fast which extends beyond three days.

That intense hunger first felt will gradually leave after the first 24 - 36hrs, but returns when all the fat reserves have been completely used up, at this point the fast should be discontinued.

The first step before you begin your fasting

The first step I would urge you to do is to talk to your doctor, (but be warned, not all doctors are trained in this area and may possess limited understanding of fasting). But the wisest choice still, is to have a thorough check up (physical examination) to ensure you are in good health. By taking an examination, you may discover you have a physical condition that makes fasting unsafe or dangerous. And also, if you are on medication, be sure to have a talk with your doctor before making the step.

Examples of persons who should not fast without doctors' advice, and/or professional supervision

" Woman who are pregnant or nursing

" Anyone with tumors, bleeding ulcers, cancer, blood diseases, or heart disease

" If you suffer from chronic problem with kidneys, liver, lungs, heart, and other organs

" Persons who are taking insulin for diabetes, or suffer from other blood sugar problem such as hyperglycemia.

Even if you fall in the above mentioned category, don't be discouraged, like I said, first go and get a checkup from your doctor.

It would also be better if such persons' part-takes in a supervised "fasting weight loss" program, where the fasting is monitored by a trained individual (there are therapeutic fasting centers that offer this service for a charge). But remember to first check with your doctor before taking that route.

How does "fasting for weight loss" works?

When you fast, you take a break from the consumption of food thus giving your body a rest, allowing accumulated toxic waste matters to be removed. That's why liquid in-take becomes necessary, because it speeds up the detoxification process allowing toxins to be eliminated and excreted from the body mainly through urination.

The byproduct of this method of detoxification is the removal and reduction of unhealthy body fat, hence producing significant weight loss.

How much weight can I expect to lose?

Weight loss through fasting depends on two things: how quick your body takes to purge itself, and the length of the fast. For some people, they will start seeing results in as little as three days, while with others, it may require a longer length of time or several phases of fasting to see significant weight reduction.

But to retain and maintain the obtained benefits of fasting weight loss, it is important that you first rid your body of parasite by taking a parasite cleanse, then stick to a balance and nutritious diet that will help you to have less toxic build up in your body allowing you to keep a stable weight.

Fasting for weight loss is without a doubt one of the best methods of losing weight, because it leads to the elimination of poisonous toxins from your body and restores your health; but as effective as it has proven to be, it should also be accompanied by a "parasite cleanse" to ensure the "benefits of fasting" isn't lost.

FASTING FOR WOMEN

For women who are interested in weight loss, intermittent fasting may seem like a great choice, but many people want to know, should women fast? Is intermittent fasting effective for women? There have been a few key studies about intermittent fasting which can help to shed some light on this interesting new dietary trend.

Intermittent fasting is also known as alternate-day fasting, although there are certainly some variations on this diet. The American Journal of Clinical Nutrition performed a study recently that enrolled 16 obese men and women on a 10-week program.

On the fasting days, participants consumed food to 25% of their estimated energy needs. The rest of the time, they received dietary counseling, but were not given a specific guideline to follow during this time.

As expected, the participants lost weight due to this study, but what researchers really found interesting were some specific changes. The subjects were all still obese after just 10 weeks, but they had shown improvement in cholesterol, LDL-cholesterol, triglycerides, and systolic blood pressure.

What made this an interesting find was that most people have to lose more weight than these study participants before seeing the same changes. It was a fascinating find which has spurred a great number of people to try fasting.

Intermittent fasting for women has some beneficial effects. What makes it especially important for women who are trying to lose weight is that women have a much higher fat proportion in their bodies. When trying to lose weight, the body mainly burns through carbohydrate stores with the first 6 hours and then starts to burn fat. Women who are following a healthy diet and exercise plan may be struggling with tenacious fat, but fasting is a realistic resolution to this.

Intermittent Fasting for Women Over 50

Obviously our physiques and our metabolism changes when we hit menopause. One of the biggest transformations that women over 50 experience is that they have a slower metabolism and they begin to put on weight. Fasting may be a good way to reverse and prevent this weight gain though.

Research have shown that this fasting pattern assists to regulate appetite and people who follow it regularly do not experience the same cravings that others do. If you're over 50 and trying to adjust to your dimmer metabolism, intermittent fasting can help you to avoid eating too much on a day-to-day basis.

When you reach 50, your body also starts to develop some chronic diseases like high cholesterol and abnormal blood pressure. Intermittent fasting has been shown to decrease both cholesterol and blood pressure, even without a great deal of weight loss.

If you've started to notice your numbers rising at the doctor's office each year, you may be able to bring them back down with fasting, even without losing much weight.

Intermittent fasting may not be a great idea for every woman. Anyone with a specific health condition or who tends to be hypoglycemic should consult with a doctor. However, this new alimentary trend has specific benefits for women who naturally store more fat in their bodies and may have trouble getting rid of these fat stores.

Both men and women scuffle with weight problems. However, women are more eager when it comes to keeping their looks. It is the dream of every woman to have a perfect body that looks good in any and every clothing.

This makes losing weight more serious for women as they want to look their best at all times. The good news about losing weight is that there are several methods to make the process faster and easier.

Limit Calorie Intake

The one thing that needs to be understood clearly when it comes to losing and adding weight is that the calories are the main culprits. If you end up eating more calories than you burn, then you end up gaining weight. This makes it very important to make sure that the calories in are less than the calories out. You can simply accomplish this by restraining the amount of calories that you eat on a daily basis. It means knowing your foods and their calorie levels followed by getting the portions right. You then must make sure that you burn more calories daily. It is the secret on how to lose weight fast for women.

Move More

The accuracy is that most career women barely find time to move around. They are in most cases swamped in the office and take only very short breaks. However, easy walks can do the magic for you when it comes to losing weight. Even when at the office, try and walk about more. You can take benefit of your breaks to go for short walks which will fetch you great results with losing weight. When you are on the move, you boost the natural rate of metabolism which keeps the fats burning. The more dynamic you are throughout the day the better it will be for your weight loss goals.

Workout Regularly

Working out seems like a lot of work. The truth however is that there are very simple exercises that you can do even without having to stay at the gym. When you keep up with a regular workout regime, you will be increasing the chances of losing weight fast. You can do a run or if you have time, spend a few minutes in the gym several times a week. Working out does not only ensure that fat is kept burning at a high level, but it also helps in toning your body.

Focus More on Intense Cardio

Cardio exercises have never disappointed when it comes to losing weight. You might therefore find it more beneficial to focus especially on intense cardio sessions. They provide a simple way of elevating the metabolism and burning calories. The best thing about cardio exercises is that the activities are fun and exciting. You will therefore enjoy your sessions more thus getting most out of it. Some of the intense exercises that you can focus on include indoor riding, running, swimming and gap training.

A STEP BY STEP GUIDE TO INTERMITTENT FASTING FOR WOMEN OVER 50

Intermittent fasting is pretty simple.

At bottom, you don't eat for most of the day, then you cram all of your calories into an "eating window" that can last anywhere from a couple to 6 to 8 hours.

If that sounds stupid, uncomfortable, or even unhealthy, I understand. I thought the same thing when I first heard about it years ago.

It turns out, though, that it's not like other fad diets. It's not going to go the way of the grapefruit diet, "detox" cleanses, and the dodo bird.

On the contrary, intermittent fasting can be an effective tool for refining nutritional compliance, it has good science on its side, and it doesn't have to be unpleasant.

In fact, many people enjoy IF more than traditional eating patterns, mainly because it allows you to have larger meals.

What IF isn't, though, is a phenomenon maker.

It won't automagically help you gain muscle and lose fat at the same time, burn away that belly fat, or stay young forever.

As you'll learn in this book, the fundamentals of appropriate dieting still very much apply, and the main reason to do it is simply because you like it.

It isn't complicated, either. There are just 5 simple steps to getting started:

Let's take a look at each.

Step 1. Choose which protocol you want to follow.

Intermittent fasting has really taken off in recent years, and there are several popular schedules to choose from.

The ones you'll hear the most about in fitness circles are Leangains, Eat Stop Eat, The Warrior Diet, and alternate-day fasting.

There are many others, of course, but all that I've seen are just derivatives of the above, and thus aren't worth mentioning.

Let's take a closer look at each of those above, and see what will best fit your needs.

Leangains is an intermittent fasting diet created and popularized by Martin Berkhan.

It was designed specifically for weightlifters and people who care about their body composition, and it's why IF has gained so much traction in the bodybuilding section.

It's also my personal favorite out of the bunch because it's simple, effective, and doesn't involve tremendously long fasts.

Here's how it works:

- Women above should fast for 14 hours and eat food in the remaining 10 hours.
- The fast starts after you've eaten your last meal of the day, and ends with your first meal of the day.
- You aren't supposed to eat or drink any calories during the fast, but black coffee, zero-calorie sweeteners, diet soda, and sugar-free gum are allowed.

So, for example, if you're a woman and you eat your last meal at 9 PM at night, then you won't eat your next meal until 1 PM the following day. If you're a woman, you break your fast two hours' sooner, at 11 AM.

As you can see, Leangains more or less boils down to "skip breakfast," which many people like to do anyway.

Step 2. Calculate your calories.

You may have heard that you don't have to watch your calories with intermittent fasting.

This is absolutely false.

No matter what type of diet you follow, caloric intake is always king.

If you want to lose weight, you need to eat fewer calories than you burn, and if you want to gain weight, you need to eat more.

End of story.

That said, intermittent fasting may help you better control your caloric intake by making the overall experience of dieting more enjoyable. The better you can stick to the plan, the better your results will be in the long run.

Step 3. Calculate your macronutrients.

You've probably heard that not all calories are identical. That "a calorie isn't a calorie."

This isn't true if all you want to do is loss or gain weight.

If, however, you want to lose fat and not muscle (or gain muscle and not fat), then it's very true. Some calories are more important than others.

For example, ...

• Eating enough protein helps you better recover from your workouts, preserve muscle while dieting, control hunger, and gain muscle effectively.
• Eating enough carbs helps you perform better in your workouts and gain muscle faster.
• Eating enough fat promotes a healthy hormone profile, helps you better absorb the nutrients you eat and have healthy skin and hair.
• That's why you have to do more than getting your calories right. You have to get your "macros" right, too (eat the right amounts of protein, carbs, and fat).

And how do you do that, exactly?

Let's start by figuring out your protein intake.

- If your goal is to lose fat, research shows that you should eat about 1 to 1.2 grams of protein per pound of body weight per day for the best results.

  If you're very overweight (25%+ body fat in men and 30%+ in women), then you can drop your protein intake to 1 gram per pound of lean body mass.
- If you want to gain or maintain your weight, then 1 gram of protein per pound of body weight per day is sufficient.

  You should then calculate your fat intake next.
- If you want to lose fat, eat between 0.2 and 0.25 grams of fat per pound of body weight per day.
- For maintenance or muscle gain, bump that up to 0.3 to 0.35 grams per pound per day.

That leaves your carbs, which should simply comprise your remaining calories for the day (30 to 50% of total daily calories for most people).

Step 4. Create a meal plan that works.

Your efforts to build your best body ever can be thwarted by stupidly simple things.

Not having the right foods at home, for example. Or being too restrictive with the foods you "allow" yourself to eat. Or accidentally eating more calories that you mean to.

That's why I recommend you become skilled at meal planning. It's the simplest way to guarantee results in the gym.

A meal plan is exactly what it sounds like: a plan for what you're going to eat and when.

It doesn't have be boring, restrictive, or inconvenient, either. In fact, a good meal plan is the complete opposite. You should look forward to your meals, you should eat the foods you like, and it should never feel burdensome.

Step 5. Train while fasted.

At this point, you may be wondering how exercise fits into all of this.

Well, many people that do intermittent fasting also do a lot of "fasted training."

Many people mistakenly think these are the same thing, but they're not. When we're talking intermittent fasting, we're talking about when we eat. Fasted training, on the other hand, is when we exercise.

Basically, if you exercise after having fasted (real fasting, by the way— no food or calories) for 5 to 6 hours, it's fasted training.

Your insulin levels are low, and your body is relying solely on its power stores to stay alive.

On the other hand, if you exercise after having eaten in the last few hours, it's "fed" training because insulin levels are lofty and your body is running at least partly on energy obtained from the meal.

Now, you don't have to train while fasting if you're doing IF (you can work out after breaking your fast), but you may find it more convenient.

Many people doing IF like to work out first thing in the morning, and break their fasts afterward with a big post-workout meal.

Many people also like to do fasted training while cutting, because it helps you burn more fat in your workouts, and especially "stubborn fat" that clings to your abs, hips, and thighs.

You can also combine it with a few supplement to further amplify these fat-burning advantages.

For women who have an interest in weight loss, intermittent fasting may appear like a terrific option, but many people would like to know, should ladies fast? Is intermittent fasting effective for women? There have been a couple of key research studies about intermittent fasting which can assist to shed some light on this interesting brand-new dietary trend.

Intermittent fasting is likewise known as alternate-day fasting, although there are certainly some variations on this diet. On the fasting days, participants consumed food to 25% of their approximated energy requirements.

What made this an interesting find was that a lot of people have to lose more weight than these study individuals prior to seeing the exact same modifications. It was a fascinating discover which has actually spurred a fantastic number of people to try fasting.

Intermittent fasting for females has some beneficial effects. What makes it specifically important for women who are trying to drop weight is that ladies have a much higher fat proportion in their bodies. When trying to lose weight, the body primarily burns through carbohydrate stores with the first 6 hours and after that starts to burn fat. Women who are following a healthy diet plan and workout strategy may be dealing with stubborn fat, but fasting is a practical option to this.

Intermittent Fasting For Women Over 50

Certainly our bodies and our metabolism changes when we hit menopause. One of the greatest modifications that ladies over 50 experience is that they have a slower metabolic process and they start to gain weight. Fasting may be an excellent way to reverse and prevent this weight gain. Research studies have shown that this fasting pattern helps to manage cravings and people who follow it routinely do not experience the exact same cravings that others do. If you're over 50 and attempting to adjust to your slower metabolic process, intermittent fasting can assist you to avoid consuming excessive on a daily basis.

When you reach 50, your body also starts to develop some persistent illness like high cholesterol and high blood pressure. Intermittent fasting has actually been shown to reduce both cholesterol and blood pressure, even without a good deal of weight-loss. If you have actually begun to observe your numbers rising at the medical professional's office each year, you might have the ability to bring them pull back with fasting, even without losing much weight.

Intermittent fasting may not be a terrific idea for each lady. Anybody with a particular health condition or who tends to be hypoglycemic ought to speak with a doctor. However, this new dietary pattern has specific advantages for females who naturally save more fat in their bodies and might have problem eliminating these fat stores.

CHAPTER 3 :

THE BASICS OF EATING DURING INTERMITTENT FASTING

T
he nutrition you follow whilst Intermittent Fasting will be determined by the results that you are looking for and where you are starting out from as well, so take a look at yourself and ask the question what do I want from this?

If you are looking to lose an important amount of weight then you are really going to have to take a look at your diet more closely, but if you just want to lose a few pounds for the beach then you may find that a few weeks of intermittent fasting can do that for you.

Although there are several different ways you can do intermittent fasting we are only going to look at the 24 hour fasting system which is what I used to lose 27 pounds over a 2-month period. The basic method is to fast twice a week for 24 hours, it makes sense to do this a few days apart and it is easier if you pick a day when you are busy so that you do not become distracted by feelings of famine.

Initially you may feel some hunger pangs but these will pass and as you become more accustomed to intermittent fasting you may find as I have that feelings of hunger no longer present you with a difficulty. You may find that you have great focus and concentration whilst fasting which is the other side of what you would expect but many people experience this.

While fasting you can and should drink plenty of water to avoid dehydration, tea and coffee are okay as long as you only take a splash of milk. If you are concerned that you are not getting enough nutrients into your body then you might consider a juice made from celery, broccoli, ginger and lime which will taste great and get some nutrient rich liquid into your body. Although if you can administer it then it would be best to stick to the water, tea and coffee.

Whatever your diet is whether it's nourishing or not you should see weight loss after about 3 weeks of intermittent fasting and do not be discouraged if you don't notice much progress at first, it's not a race and it's better to lose weight in a straight fashion over time rather than crash losing a few pounds which you will put straight back on.

After the first month you may want to take a look at your diet on non-fasting days and cut out high sugar foods and any jumble that you may normally eat. I have found that intermittent fasting over the long term tends to make me want to eat healthier foods as a natural course.

If you are intermittent fasting for bodybuilding then you may want to consider looking at your macro nutrients and working out how much protein and carbohydrate you need to eat, this is much more complicated and you can find information about this on several websites which you will need to spend time researching for the best results.

There are many benefits to intermittent fasting which you will notice as you progress, some of these benefits include more energy, less bloating, a clearer mind and a general feeling of wellness.

It's important not to succumb to any temptation to binge eat after a fasting period as this will negate the effect gained from the intermittent fasting period.

THE BASICS OF INTERMITTENT FASTING

Over the years there have been several studies conducted and experiments done to find the effectiveness of weight loss through intermittent fasting.

The term intermittent fasting basically means splitting up the day in zones, there will be eating zones and others will be fasting zones. More popularly known as eating windows and fasting, the key is maintaining the fraction and working in the spaces while doing it.

Weight loss by this medium is simpler than hefty workouts or specially breastfeeding moms who cannot afford the time to manage a gym or workout. Intermittent fasting is just what people want to do, eat whatever one wants to have that is chocolates, cream and other fat products and let the calories go into deficit.

It is no secret that intermittent fasting helps rejuvenate the body and the fitness of a person, during intermittent fasting the person consumes only water, juices, or other low calorie elements. It signifies a period of eating followed by a period of non-eating. However, having water alone during the fasting helps to clean the body and drive out the filths inside the body.

In many cultures especially the Chinese intermittent fasting is more or less made compulsory to everyone, which enable people from those parts of the world to be highly agile and fit.

To get the hang of intermittent fasting and how weight loss occurs with its convention in daily life-style, here is a quick summary of how to practice it and take benefit from it-

1) Choose the 24 hours IF technique or 12-hour window

There are several types of intermittent fasting agendas that can be decided on, some vary from 24 hours plus which means eating on Tuesday 6pm and then taking the next meal on Wednesday 6pm. A fast that long should not be promoted as such since it affects the metabolic rate and in turn health deteriorates.

The better option is to choose a 12-hour window, where fasting is done for half a day and then any fat or carbohydrate food which is beneficial for the body. What happens is when one meal is taken, the body uses it till the next 12 hours and when it is digested the calorie which is stored as fat is burnt and used by the body. Weight loss takes place with that and after some time the urge and hunger pangs also disappear as the body gets used to it.

2) Keep the diet simple and short

Weight loss through intermittent fasting only happens when it is practiced consistently. For consistency there should be a plan that is simple and easily followed on a daily basis. Fix food groups on 12 hours' intervals and just have those.

Balancing the groups in meek ways would determine the intake of food which is vital for the body's well-being, good metabolism and eventually weight burning out in a way unforeseen. The group can have calcium, fiber, carbohydrates and fats. The only thing is to balance it applicably.

3) Reduces stress on the body needing to snack time and again

Intermittent fasting basically molds the body needs in a way where needs of frequent snacking automatically die down. So what happens is the time when extra meal intake and fat used to store in the body, that particular time is simply chopped off from the daily routine and weight loss starts happening with this.

The stress that the body took in processing, digesting and using the fat and extra meal in take is also reduced, instead the same amount of energy is used in digesting the stored calories and burns it down by reducing fat on stomach and other parts of the body.

4) Blood sugar levels and routines are adjusted appropriately

With intermittent fasting there are various advantages to health factors, and one of them is balanced blood sugar levels as the intake in the body reduces.

Analyses show that lesser cravings happen and apart from sugar level, blood pressure, stress and heart diseases are also taken under regulator through this form of dieting. So not only would rigorous workouts be avoided and tough food cuts would not take place, eating just about everything one desires and still reducing weight happens in a span of few months.

Moreover, there are healthier and nutrients food intake developed over a period of time which when IF is not followed is tough to make a habit of.

Intermittent fasting bodybuilding and the joy of it

Fasting and bodybuilding are often related to each other, in order to build the body, it is highly essential that the body be fit, for the body to be fit, one of the natural ways or the most effective way is intermittent fasting, as it helps in lashing away the impurities of the body and gives the various organs that participate in the digestion of food their quota of much needed rest.

Hence the person will start feeling more and more cozy and happy with himself, this incoming feeling of wellness induces the self-reliance in the person and motivates him to build the body. Intermittent fasting bodybuilding hence is a natural way of improving ones fitness levels.

Points to be taken care of during intermittent fasting bodybuilding

1. For novices the concept of intermittent fasting bodybuilding may seem to be a Herculean task, and may easily give up in no time, but it has to be understood that fasting at regular intervals of time helps oneself and boosts his self-assurance over a period of time. The determination has to be maintained in order to get the optimum results.

2. There is another drift which we should be very wary of, and it is not to go overboard and strain yourself. Often people in a hurry to get fit and build the body of their dreams, fast too much that they fall sick, it should be avoided.

3. This can be avoided by keeping an eye out for the various hints and clues the body gives you. Like you should go and eat something and some food once you start feeling very light-headed or a bit too tired or any other symbols that the body sends to indicate that it's in dire need of some calories.

There is no point in fasting for a while and then shoving yourself with calories immediately after you have finished your fasting, instead slowly start taking in calories and exercise in the desired manner, making sure not to hurt yourself or overdo the exercises.

Fasting & bodybuilding are one of the oldest and the time tested methods of purifying one's own body and hence maintain it in proper condition. This helps you maintain your body in shape and also gives you the much needed confidence about yourself, above all it makes you realize the value of food and the importance of it.

Similarly, it also forms one of the basic building blocks for body building, since for building a body it is essential that you have a conditioned body, if the body is not in a proper condition then it has to be brought to proper condition using the age old method of intermittent fasting and then build it.

THE BASICS OF EXERCISE ON INTERMITTENT FASTING

Scroll through any social media platform or online health and fitness publication, and you're bound to read about someone doing intermittent fasting (IF) while still maintaining their exercise routine.

While the attention the IF craze is getting seems to be over the top, this type of lifestyle isn't new. There's decent findings and anecdotal reports about how to make IF work especially if you're scheduling to exercise while doing it.

Intermittent fasting has picked up quite a bit of steam in the health world, as people who experiment with it have seen remarkable results: improved energy levels, stable blood sugar, weight loss, and more. In a world where we reach for a snack every two hours, it makes sense that our bodies welcome the natural fasting arrangements of our lineages.

But what does exercise look like during a fast? That depends on a variety of factors, from the fast you choose some people fast for 16 hours and eat for eight daily, while others eat between 500 and 600 calories on two nonconsecutive days of the week to how your body responds to it.

It's important to listen to your body, If you feel too weak to work out from fasting, then you should take care of your nutrition and work out later.

While safety should always come first, a variety of workouts are excellent complements to IF. Here's what you need to know.

Can you exercise while on a fast?

If you're trying IF or you're fasting for other reasons and you still want to get your workouts in, there are some pros and cons to consider before you decide to work out in a fasted state.

Some research shows that exercising while fasting affects muscle biochemistry and metabolism that's linked to insulin sensitivity and the steady control of blood sugar levels. Research also supports eating and immediately exercising before digestion or absorption occurs. This is particularly important for anyone with type 2 diabetes or metabolic syndrome.

Does the potential to burn more fat sound like a win? Before you jump on the fasted cardio trend, there's a downside.

Plan your meals around your workouts.

Professional often recommends cardio on an empty stomach, so booking that early morning spin class or going for a jog works well if you're fasting. But choosing the right foods the night before is crucial.

"Knowing you're going to exercise, you should be thinking about what to eat the day before, depending on the intensity of the workout. For example, you may want to figure your glycogen stores with complex carbs for dinner the night before so that you have readily available energy for a cardio workout,".

You never want to do cardio on a full stomach, as the sudden demand for blood flow from the muscles will steal vital blood flow needed by the digestive system for digestion and assimilation of nutrients.

The key is to plan ahead so your nutrition can meet the demands required by the intensity of your workout, even when it's the next morning."

HOW CAN YOU SAFELY EXERCISE WHILE FASTING?

The success of any weight loss or exercise program depends on how safe it is to sustain over time. If your ultimate goal is to decrease body fat and maintain your fitness level while doing IF, you need to stay in the safe zone. Here are some expert tips to help you do just that.

Eat a meal close to your moderate- to high-intensity workout

This is where meal timing comes into play. Khorana says that timing a meal close to a moderate- or high-intensity workout is key. This way your body has some glycogen stores to tap into to fuel your workout.

Stay hydrated

To remember fasting doesn't mean to remove water. In fact, he recommends that you drink more water while fasting.

Keep your electrolytes up

A good low-calorie hydration source, is coconut water. "It replenishes electrolytes, is low in calories, and tastes pretty good," he says. Gatorade and sports drinks are high in sugar, so avoid drinking too much of them.

Keep the intensity and duration fairly low If you push yourself too hard and begin to feel dizzy or light-headed, take a break. Listening to your body is important.

Consider the type of fast

If you're doing a 24-hour intermittent fast, you should stick to low-intensity workouts such as walking, restorative yoga, or gentle Pilates. But if you're doing the 16:8 fast, much of the 16-hour fasting window is evening, sleep, and early in the day, so sticking to a certain type of exercise isn't as critical.

Listen to your body

The most important advice to heed when exercising during IF is to listen to your body. "If you start to feel weak or dizzy, chances are you're experiencing low blood sugar or are dehydrated,". If that's the case, she says to opt for a carbohydrate-electrolyte drink immediately and then follow up with a well-balanced meal.

While exercising and intermittent fasting may work for some people, others may not feel comfortable doing any form of exercise while fasting. Check with your doctor or healthcare provider before starting any nutrition or exercise program.

THE BASICS OF EATING ON INTERMITTENT FASTING

There may be a lot of readers who are only familiar with one or the other. Both have a special style that packs a big punch to fat loss and proper health. On the surface only one of them is considered a "diet," but even that term is held very loosely. I am very familiar with both of them in regards to fat loss and overall health benefits so to give an overall summary for both will be suitable. I truly believe that if you bridge the gap and combine these two styles, you will be able to produce some pretty amazing fat loss results. Let's begin!

Fasting for Fat Loss Is Extremely Effective

The idea of fasting in a diet plan tends to get very negative remarks within the fitness culture. Many companies and trainers have us believing that if you aren't eating every few hours than your metabolism will slow down or cause our bodies to go into "starvation mode." Before we go any further, we must establish that "slowing of the metabolism" may be one of the biggest myths in the entire fitness industry. Metabolism is decreased under chronic, low-calorie consumptions that last weeks on end.

This does not happen when fasting is done a couple times a week. Here is a simple outline of how intermittent fasting is applied into someone's schedule. I'll explain how this can be tweaked to your liking later.

1. Eat normal until dinner (2-4 meals, not 6-8)
2. Eat your dinner but stop eating after that.
3. Fast until dinner the following day. (No calorie consumption)

4. For that meal just eat a regular size dinner.

In this approach you are still fasting for a 24-hour period, but are still having a meal every day. This is done typically 1-2 times a week. If you need to drop a lot of weight before a vacation or reunion, then you can fast 3 times a week. I would only recommend this for a few weeks.

What You Learn About Yourself During Fasting

When fasting, you will want to take note of any changes in the way you eat. Once you have completed a 24 hour fast a few times, the reasons of what, when, and why you eat may be revealed to you. A lot of the reasons why we eat is because of emotional connections or pure habit and not with actual hunger itself. Sometimes we are so conditioned to eat at certain times that we consume a meal when we aren't hungry.

Intermittent Fasting Is a Lifestyle And Not A Diet

The reason why it is not considered a "diet" is because it doesn't restrict you to certain foods, recipes, combinations, instructions, or charts to follow in order to lose weight. It rids you of neurotic compulsive eating habits and allows you variety. Instead of completely avoiding a particular food because someone told you to, adding a variety of foods will actually prevent you from over-eating any type of "bad" food.

Now that we have established this area of fat loss, let's turn to a deeper issue in regards to diet and health.

What Is the Phase One Diet AKA The Fungus Link?

Doug Kaufmann is the mastermind behind the idea of fungus and yeast contributing to bad health and weight loss failures. He has researched and documented how fungi produces venomous substances called "mycotoxins" which causes many health problems. He tackles the problem by addressing areas where fungi and yeast can enter the body, but also provides the solution in starving the fungus to reverse the symptoms of so many health problems in America.

He has found that fungi, like people, crave specific carbohydrates. Knowing that fungi must have carbohydrates in order to thrive inside the body makes the Phase 1 Diet understandable to use.

So What Is Allowed On the Phase 1 Diet?

This is the only "diet" that I would ever recommend that actually restricts certain types of food, but for a specific reason. The exclusion of certain foods is done momentarily to starve and kill the fungus as well as exposing the root of food cravings. Food cravings that are not under control can be detrimental to your health as well as the added pounds on the belly, thighs, hips, you name it.

Fungus overgrowth may in fact be the root failure in losing the weight. As long as you are addicted to certain foods you will continue to eat and eat unconsciously. Many people find that their health elevates to a level where they can't believe how great they feel. A large reason for this is because of the specific food choice that starves and prevents overgrowth of fungus. Many people are living better because of this breakthrough approach to eating. Here is a quick outline of food choices that are suitable on the Phase 1 Diet.

EXAMPLE OF ACCEPTABLE FOODS FOR THE PHASE 1 DIET

1)Eggs

2)FRUIT: Berries, Grapefruit, Lemon, Lime, Green Apples, Avocado, Fresh Coconut

3)MEATS: Virtually all meat including fish, poultry and beef

4)VEGETABLES: Fresh, unblemished vegetables and freshly made vegetable juice

5)BEVERAGES: Bottled or filtered water, non-fruity herbal teas, stevia sweetened fresh lemonade, freshly squeezed carrot juice.

6)VINEGAR: apple cider vinegar

7)OILS: olive, grape, flax seed, cold pressed virgin coconut oil

8)NUTS: raw nuts, including pecans, almonds, walnuts, cashews, and pumpkin seeds. Stored nuts tend to gather mold, so be careful!

9)SWEETENERS: Stevia, Xylitol

10)DAIRY: Organic Butter, Organic Yogurt, (use the following very sparingly) cream cheese, unsweetened whipping cream, real sour cream.

TYPES OF FOODS FOR INTERMITTENT FASTING

Of all the fad diets of the moment, intermittent fasting has garnered much attention for its convincing evidence in scientific literature. Throughout history, fasting has been utilized as an expression of political dissent, desire for spiritual reward, as well as a therapeutic tool, but only recently has it gained widespread traction among fitness gurus for its touted weight loss and anti-aging effects.

But that brings the big question: is there an ultimate intermittent fasting guide so you know what to eat while you're on this diet?

First, let's take a step back and break down the basics: How does the diet work when it comes to these major intermittent fasting health benefits?

Scientists postulate that the anti-aging benefits are largely due to increased insulin sensitivity, and weight loss is related to an overall reduced calorie intake because of a shortened feeding window. Simply put, when you have less time during the day to eat, you eat less. Easy, right? But a key concept, as with any diet, is determining feasibility for your lifestyle.

One recent The Lancet Diabetes & Endocrinology study showed diet-induced weight loss typically leads to a 70 percent regain in weight, so finding any type of weight-loss plan that works best for you and won't cause you any destruction in the future is the key.

Fasting from 9 p.m. until about 1 p.m. the next day works well because most people are already skipping breakfast or are eating poor ones. This method can work well around a day job, but also emphasizes the importance of maintaining dietary needs around this time restricted feeding window.

This means that overall diet quality and habitual food choices still matter while intermittent fasting and that you probably won't get the body of your dreams while chowing down on nothing but hamburgers and fries.

In fact, eating junk food in a condensed feeding window on the IF diet may actually put you at risk of a shortfall of key nutrients such as calcium, iron, protein, and fiber, all of which are essential for normal biological function.

Plus, eating a diet rich in fruits and vegetables allows for more antioxidants in your body, which, like the metabolic effects of intermittent fasting, may subsidize to a longer lifespan!

For starters, here's a breakdown of typical intermittent fasting schedules:

- Alternate Day Fasting (ADF)—1-day ad libitum eating (normal eating) alternated with 1-day complete fasting
- Modified Alternate Day Fasting (mADF)—1-day ad libitum feeding alternated with 1 day very low-calorie diet (about 25 percent of normal caloric intake)
- 2/5—Complete fasting on 2 days of the week with 5 days' ad libitum eating
- 1/6—Complete fasting on 1 day of the week with 6 days' ad libitum eating
- Time Restricting Feeding (TRF)—Fasting for 12-20 hours per day (as a prolongation of the nighttime fast) on each day of the week. "Feeding window" of 4-12 hours.

OK, so you have the time windows for when you can chow down, but you're probably wondering what to eat during your IF journey. We rounded up 19 of the best foods to create the ultimate intermittent fasting food guide that will help prevent nutrient shortfalls!

1. Water

One of the most important aspects of maintaining a healthy eating pattern while intermittent fasting is to promote hydration. As we go without fuel for 12-16 hours, our body's preferred energy source is the sugar stored in the liver, also known as glycogen.

As this energy is burned, so disappears a large volume of fluid and electrolytes. Drinking 8+ cups of water per day will prevent dehydration and also promote better blood flow, cognition, and muscle and joint support during your intermittent fasting regimen.

2. Coffee

What about a warm cup of Joe? Will a daily Starbucks run break the fast? It's a common question among newbie intermittent fasters, but worry not: coffee is allowed. Because in its natural state coffee is a calorie-free beverage, it can even technically be consumed outside a designated feeding window, but the minute syrups, creamers, or candied flavorings are added, it can no longer be consumed during the time of the fast, so that's something to keep in mind if you frequently doctor up your drink.

3. Minimally-Processed Grains

Carbohydrates are an essential part of life and are most definitely not the enemy when it comes to weight loss. Because a large chunk of your day will be spent fasting during this diet, it is important to think strategically about ways to get enough calories while not feeling overly full.

Though a healthy diet minimizes processed foods, there can be a time and place for items like whole grain breads, bagels, and crackers, as these foods are more quickly digested for fast and easy fuel. If you intend to exercise or train recurrently while intermittent fasting, these will especially be a great source of energy on the go.

4. Raspberries

Fiber the stuff that keeps you regular was named a shortfall nutrient by the 2015-2020 Dietary Guidelines, less than 10 percent of Western populations consume adequate levels of whole fruits. With 8 grams of fiber per cup, raspberries are a pleasant high fiber fruit to keep you regular during your shortened feeding window.

5. Lentils

This wholesome superstar packs a high fiber punch with 32 percent of total daily fiber needs met in only half a cup. Additionally, lentils provide a good source of iron (about 15 percent of your daily needs), another nutrient of anxiety, especially for active females undergoing intermittent fasting.

6. Potatoes

Similar to breads, white potatoes are digested with minimal effort from the body, and if paired with a protein source, they are a perfect post-workout snack to refuel hungry muscles. Another grant making potatoes an indispensable staple for the IF diet is that once cooled, potatoes form a resistant starch primed to fuel good bacteria in your gut.

7. Seitan

The EAT-Lancet Commission recently released a report calling for a dramatic reduction in animal-based proteins for optimal health and longevity. One large study directly linked consumption of red meat to increased mortality.

Make the most of your anti-aging fast by incorporating life-extending plant-based protein substitutes like seitan. Also known as "wheat meat," this food can be battered, baked, and dipped in your favorite sauces.

8. Hummus

One of the creamiest and tastiest dips known to mankind, hummus is another excellent plant-based protein and is a great way to boost nutritional content of staples like sandwiches (just sub for mayonnaise!) If you're courageous enough to make your own, don't forget the secret to the perfect recipe is ample garlic and tahini.

9. Wild-Caught Salmon

If your goal is to be a member of the centenarian club, you might want to read up on the Blue Zones. These five geographical regions in Europe, Latin America, Asia, and the U.S. are well known for dietary and lifestyle choices linked to extreme longevity. One commonly consumed food across these zones is salmon, which is high in brain-boosting omega-3 fatty acids EPA and DHA.

10. Soybeans

As if we needed another excuse to splurge for an appetizer at the sushi bar, is flavones, one of the active compounds in soybeans, have verified to inhibit UVB induced cell damage and stimulate anti-aging. So, next time you host a dinner party in, astonish your guests with a delicious recipe featuring soybeans!

11. Multivitamins

One of the proposed mechanisms behind why IF leads to weight loss is due to the fact that the individual simply has less time to eat and therefore eats less. While the principle of energy in versus energy out holds true, something that isn't often discussed is the risk of vitamin shortages while in a caloric deficit. Though a multivitamin is not necessary with a balanced diet of plenty of fruits and vegetables, life can get hectic, and a supplement can help fill the gaps.

12. Smoothies

If a daily supplement doesn't sound appealing, try springing for a double dose of vitamins by creating homemade smoothies packed with fruits and vegetables. Smoothies are a great way to consume multiple different foods, each uniquely packed with different essential nutrients.

Quick tip: Buying frozen can help save money and ensure ultimate freshness.

13. Vitamin D Fortified Milk

The recommended intake of calcium for an adult is 1,000 milligrams per day, or in plain speak, 3 cups of milk per day. With a reduced feeding window, chances to drink this much might be scarce, and so it is important to prioritize high calcium foods. Vitamin D fortified milk enhances the body's absorption of calcium and will help to keep bones strong. To boost daily calcium intake, you can add milk to smoothies or cereal, or even just drink it with meals. If you're not a fan of the beverage, non-dairy sources high in calcium include tofu and soy products, as well as leafy greens like kale.

14. Red Wine

A glass of wine and a night of beauty sleep may keep heads turning, as the polyphenol found in grapes has distinct anti-aging effects. Humans are known to have one of the enzyme classes SIRT-1, which is thought to act upon resveratrol in the presence of a caloric deficit to enhance both insulin sensitivity and longevity.

15. Blueberries

Don't let their miniature size fool you: Blueberries are proof that good things come in small packages! Studies have shown that longevity and youthfulness is a result of anti-oxidative processes. Blueberries are a great source of antioxidants and wild blueberries are even one of the highest sources of antioxidants. Antioxidants help rid the body of free radicals and prevent widespread cellular damage.

16. Papaya

During the final hours of your fast, you'll likely start to feel the effects of hunger, especially as you first start intermittent fasting. This "hanger" may, in turn, cause you to overeat in large quantities, leaving you feeling bloated and lethargic minutes later. Papaya possesses a unique enzyme called papain that acts upon proteins to break them down. Including chunks of this tropical fruit in a protein-dense meal can help ease digestion, making any bloat more manageable.

17. Nuts

Make room on the cheese board for a mixed assortment, because nuts of all varieties are known to rid body fat and lengthen your life. A prospective trial published in the British Journal of Nutrition even associated nut consumption with a reduced risk of cardiovascular disease, type 2 diabetes, and overall mortality.

18. Ghee

Of course, you've heard a drizzle of olive oil has major health benefits, but there are plenty of other oil options out there you can use, too. You don't want to heat an oil you're cooking with beyond its smoke point, so next time you're in the kitchen whipping up a stir-fry, consider using ghee as your oil of choice. Basically just clarified butter, it has a much higher smoke point making it a great choice for hot dishes.

19. Homemade Salad Dressing

Just like your grandmother kept her cooking wholesome and simple, so should you when it comes to salad dressings and sauces. When we opt to make our own simple dressings, unwanted additives and extra sugar are avoided. In fact, according to a dermatological journal, sugar might be accelerating the aging process more than any other ingredient by degrading cross-linkages of collagen fibers in our skin.

TYPES OF FLUIDS FOR INTERMITTENT FASTING

"Can I drink liquids while I am fasting?" That is one of the most common questions that people have when starting off with the intermittent fasting. It can be unclear to figure out which intermittent fasting liquids are adequate, and which are not.

Can you drink as much water as you want? What about your morning cup of coffee? Will beverages like zero-calorie diet soda interfere with fat burning during fasting?

In this book, I'll answer all of those questions and more so that you can be confident knowing what to drink while fasting and what not to.

Water is the most important liquid on your list. Every single organ in your body uses water. Your blood cells carry water and oxygen to your organs, including your brain. The more water in your bloodstream, the smoother your blood flows. Water helps keep your skin supple and it also helps normalize your mood, according to the American College of Healthcare Sciences. One of the first signs of dehydration is petulance, which can not only make it harder to stay on your fast, it can place an unfair emotional burden on the people around you.

Drinking plain water can get boring, so aim for 8 to 11 cups of water per day. Vary your liquid consumption with other healthy choices such as:

- Unfiltered apple juice.
- Pure fruit juices with no added sweeteners, colors or flavors.
- Sodium-free or low sodium sparkling water.

- Soy milk and nut milks.
- Decaffeinated teas and tisanes.
- Vegetable, chicken or beef broth.

Apple cider vinegar fasting alone is not a good idea, because it does not provide your body with a full range of necessary vitamins and minerals. Unfiltered apple juice is a far better choice, because it contains a bit of fiber along with vitamin C. Juices with no added sugar, artificial colors or flavors provide pure nutrition without the chemical additives you are trying to avoid.

Fruit juices are very high in natural sugars, so it is a good idea to add protein such as yogurt to your liquid diet to help slow down the insulin response.

Sparkling water or club soda can liven up a steady stream of plain juices. Add a substantial splash of cranberry, mango, pineapple or grapefruit juice for a refreshing beverage that gives you all of the bubbly carbonation of soda without the chemicals or the calories. Read the labels to ensure that your beverage of choice is marked low sodium or sodium free.

Most fasts require you to give up dairy, which can be a challenge if you love the creaminess of an ice-cold glass of milk or prefer your tea a little less bitter.

Soy milk and nut milks are delicious substitutes for dairy. They are also a good addition to smoothies, because the protein in soy and nut milks helps slow the absorption of the natural sugars in fruit, and they can also help you feel full for longer than a smoothie made of fruit alone.

Only dried leaves of the Camellia sinensis plant can technically be called tea. Any other infusion of water and leaves or herbs is called a tisane. Tea, whether it is black, green or white, contains powerful antioxidants that help fight the free radicals responsible for certain types of cancers and the visible signs of aging.

A cup of decaffeinated tea or a tisane sweetened with honey or agave syrup is also soothing, and can help ease nerves that are jangled by giving up all of your usual treats. Drink them iced during the day for a refreshing change from plain water.

Getting enough protein during a fast can be a challenge, so adding broth to your regimen is a smart move. Vegetable broth is an excellent choice for vegetarians and vegans, and can be powered up by adding in a bit of nondairy protein powder.

Chicken and beef broths are both high in protein; bone broth, which is simmered for between 24 and 48 hours, contains protein and collagen in more concentrated amounts. Making your own helps you control the sodium levels, though low-sodium and sodium free broths are available commercially.

Which liquids are allowed with intermittent fasting?

It is important to only drink low-calorie liquids during a fasted state. They should not spike insulin, not stop fat burning, and not inhibit your weight loss efforts.

Below is a list of beverages. These are the ones that people most commonly wonder if they can include on their keto diet and intermittent fasting eating plan.

I'll let you know which are okay, which you can have a little of, and which should be avoided completely if you want to see true benefits like weight loss and better health.

1. Tea.

Drinking small quantities of tea won't be a problem while intermittent fasting. But be aware that many teas do contain caffeine. Slight amounts of caffeine won't break fasting, but a lot of caffeine can start to stimulate insulin levels. This will get in the way of ketosis and weight loss. So limit caffeinated tea.

Non-caffeinated herbal teas are the best choice, and you can drink as much of those as you'd like.

The final verdict: Feel free to drink plenty of non-caffeinated herbal tea. Only drink small amounts of caffeinated tea.

2. Coffee.

Several people are afraid that if they start the keto diet and fasting, they will have to give up coffee completely. While I definitely don't recommend intake coffee all day long, I think it is totally fine to drink a little bit in the morning.

One cup won't be an issue. And it might help tide you over and prevent some hunger in the morning before your first meal of the day. However, too much coffee isn't good. It will rev up your adrenals, which activates cortisol and then spikes insulin.

Do not add sugar to your coffee, because this will just increase blood sugar. Xylitol is an standard alternative if you need a sweetener. A small amount of milk or cream is also acceptable, so add a splash if you prefer.

What about bulletproof coffee? Adding butter or fat to your coffee is okay for some people. But for others, that adds enough calories that the coffee starts to act like an actual meal. For some, it kicks them out of fat burning.

The final verdict: It is okay to have a cup of coffee in the morning as long as you don't add sugar and just use a small amount of cream and may be little bit of butter.

3. Water.

Drinking water will not be a problem while doing intermittent fasting. You want to stay hydrated.

When you are fasting, you will naturally lose some water and electrolytes. So it is important to keep your body replenished while doing this diet.

Consider adding some electrolytes to your water. You might be in need of salt or potassium.

You don't have to drink just straight, flat water either. Carbonation is completely fine and won't interfere with intermittent fasting at all. I love Pellegrino or other brands that are sugar free. You can even add a little bit of fresh lemon for a refreshing flavor and added health benefits. Don't have vitamin water as it comes with lot of sugar.

The final verdict: Drink plenty of water and consider adding electrolytes or lemon.

4. Diet Soda.

Because diet soda has little calories (or no calories at all), some people think it might be a good option while fasting. But diet soda is artificially sweetened. And artificial sweeteners like aspartame will absolutely increase blood sugar and spike insulin levels.

This makes it a very bad idea to drink diet soda while doing the ketogenic diet and intermittent fasting. It will definitely slow down ketosis.

If you can find diet soda sweetened only by xylitol or stevia, those can be okay. But any sodas sweetened with aspartame are off limits (which includes most sodas labeled "diet"). Even if they have no calories.

The final verdict: Do NOT drink diet soda.

5. Apple Cider Vinegar.

Apple cider vinegar is like a superfood tonic. It has so many health benefits, including helping to regulate blood sugar, decreasing the need for insulin, improving feasting, helping a fatty liver, and so much more.

This makes it one of the best intermittent fasting liquids. Choose a high quality brand. I like Bragg's organic, raw apple cider vinegar.

Combine apple cider vinegar with some water, and drink it daily for all its amazing health effects.

The final verdict: Apple cider vinegar is a very healthy fasting drink.

6. Alcohol.

You might be thinking, "Well hard liquor doesn't have calories, so it should be okay, right?" Wrong.

Alcohol acts as a toxin, kills cells, causes a fatty liver, depletes vitamins, dehydrates you, and so much more. And in terms of if it's bad for fasting? Alcohol definitely blocks fat burning, which is ultimately the goal of intermittent fasting. It will get in the way of weight loss.

Alcohol will inhibit liver function and totally knock you out of ketosis. Do not consume it.

The final verdict: Do NOT drink alcohol.

7. Coconut Water.

While it is touted as a healthy drink, coconut water is actually not very healthy. It is really high in sugar. It might be high in electrolytes, but this high sugar content is a real problem.

Any type of sugar in the diet will raise insulin, and so coconut water will definitely inhibit fat burning and be a problem for fasting. If you are looking for weight loss, ditch coconut water.

The final verdict: Do NOT drink coconut water.

8. Almond Milk.

Compared to milk and other milk alternatives, unsweetened almond milk actually doesn't have a lot of sugar or carbs in it. Rice milk, for example, has way more carbohydrates and sugar. Almond milk only has 1 gram of carbs and 0 grams of sugar in a cup. Don't drink too much of it, but a little bit here and there will not be a problem.

Just make sure that you choose an unsweetened brand. And check the other ingredients for things you might be sensitive to.

The final verdict: Unsweetened almond milk is okay in small amounts.

9. Milk.

I would not recommend drinking milk while fasting. It actually has quite a lot of sugar per serving, which will boost insulin and stop fat burning.

However, a little splash of grass-fed, organic milk in your coffee won't be a problem.

The final verdict: Don't drink a lot of milk. A splash in your morning coffee is okay.

CHAPTER 4 :

INTERMITTENT FASTING TROUBLESHOOTING

Common Mistakes When It Comes to Intermittent Fasting

The concept of intermittent fasting seems fairly honest. You withhold from eating in intervals somewhere between 16 or 20 hours a day or heavily restrict your intake and eat a very low-calorie diet a couple day a week. There are also some IF followers who eat just one meal a day (also called OMAD).

There's quite a bit of research proving that IF works for weight loss and improves things like blood sugar control and cholesterol, which are indicators for chronic diseases. Some studies have even found that IF may boost people's energy and help them sleep better.

I've been a dietitian for so many years, so I've read my share of research on IF, I've written about it a handful of times, and I've even tried intermittent fasting out for myself. Here's my take: it works really well for some people regardless of what "type" of IF they follow, but one common denominator is that plenty of folks out there are doing it wrong.

There happens to be a lot of misinformation floating around the internet (both about intermittent fasting and dieting as a whole category), so I culled a list of some of the top comments and questions on Reddit's Intermittent Fasting drift and answered them the best I could. Here are some common questions I found about IF, plus some common faults to avoid when trying it.

Some people come into difficulty with Intermittent Fasting because they approach it in the wrong way, being aware of the right procedures when undertaking Intermittent Fasting can be the difference between success and failure.

Here are the top mistakes that I see people making all the time when they are fasting:

1. You're jumping into intermittent fasting too fast.

The biggest reason most diets fail is because they're such an extreme departure from our common, natural way of eating that they often feel impossible to maintain. Just a thought, but if you're new to IF and are familiar to eating every two hours on the hour, maybe don't throw yourself into a hard-core 24-hour-fast from hell.

If you're adamant about the concept of fasting, start with some beginners 12/12 method where you're fasting for 12 hours per day and eating within the 12-hour window. That's probably pretty close to what you're used to doing anyway, and who knows, it might be the only (if even that) defensible way to follow along.

2. You're choosing the wrong plan for your lifestyle.

Again, don't set yourself up for misery by signing up for something you know is going to cramp your style. If you're a night owl, don't plan to start your fast at 6 p.m. If you're a daily gym-goer who Instagram's their WOD every morning and aren't willing to sacrifice your daily Spin, don't choose a plan that severely restricts calories a few days a week.

3. You're eating too much during the eating window.

This one is the most common trap I would expect to see people fall into with IF. If you've chosen a particularly obstructive regimen that's left you hangry AF for hours of the day, the moment the clock says "it's time to eat," you're likely to go a wee bit overboard. Research suggests restrictive diets often don't work because we tend to become so emotionally (and physically) starved that when we do allow ourselves to eat, we go hog wild and overeat in a fit of deprivation. Any diet that has you preoccupied with your next meal is a recipe for a binge so make sure you're not allowing yourself to feel unnecessarily hungry for long periods of time.

4. You're not eating enough during the eating window.

Yep, not eating enough is also legit cause of weight gain, and I'll tell you why. In addition to setting yourself up for a rebound similar to what we deliberated with the last common IF mistake, not eating enough cannibalizes your muscle mass, causing your metabolism to slow.

Without that metabolic muscle mass, you may be sabotaging your ability to maintain (never mind to lose) fat in the future. The challenge with IF is that because you're eating according to some arbitrary temporal rules, rather than listening to your body's innate cues, it's really difficult to know your true needs.

If you're adamant about doing the diet, be sure to speak to a registered dietitian to help you assess and meet your nutrient needs safely.

5. Using it as an excuse to eat rubbish.

Unfortunately, people think that intermittent fasting is a magic pill that will solve all their problems. Yes, it is an incredibly effective tool to take control of your health but it won't cancel out eating a diet full of processed foods and sugar. When you are intermittent fasting it is even more important to nourish your body with nutrient dense, whole foods.

When you are in the fasted state, your body starts to break down damaged components and then uses them for of energy, this process cleans and heals the body. It also means your body becomes more sensitive to the food you eat, this is great if it's full of nutrients to nourish the body, but not good if you are eating rubbish.

Not only that, if you aren't nourishing yourself with nutrient dense foods, you will feel hungry all the time – your body will crave nutrients.

6. You're Eating Too Many Calories.

"Does anyone else eat like crazy right when the fast is over and is it normal to have a huge appetite during the feeding period? It is hard for me to get full after a 20 hour fast and I just eat the whole 4 hours. LOL."

I'd venture to guess that this person is eating more calories than what's needed in that 4-hour window. So instead of laughing your way through a marathon all-you-can-eat session, plan for how you'll break your fast. Stock up on high-protein foods (like meats and seafood) and/or high-fiber foods (like fruits, vegetables, beans, and most whole grains). They'll not only fill you up, but will keep you feeling full.

"If I do a 20:4 fast then I should consume 1500-2000 calories within four hours? Am I understanding this correctly?"

Technically, yes. But depending on a person's body size, eating 2,000 calories in a 4-hour window might not yield any weight loss. I don't know this person's size, though. Now, most people lose weight on 1,500 calories, but one of the pros of IF is that it's hard to eat a ton of calories in a short window of time.

For some, following IF is an easier way to cut calories and lose weight than simply following a traditional calorie-restricted diet. So if you can't hit the 1,500- or 2,000-calorie mark in 4 hours every day, it's OK. If falling below 1,200 calories a day becomes a regular habit, though, reconsider your diet plan. If you're not sure how many calories you're consuming, track them in a free app like MyFitnessPal.

7. You're Overanalyzing.

"Does IF mean no food outside meal times, or no calories?"

Um, they are one in the same, no? Does anyone reading this article know of foods that have zero calories? If so, please share! This person's assumption is correct, though—no food and no calories outside of the "feeding window."

Does anyone else feel like this question comes up about a thousand times a day? Short answer: Yes. Eating anything with calories breaks your fast.

Exceptions to this rule would be black coffee, unsweetened and milk-free tea, water, and diet soda (though research says diet soda could actually increase your appetite, which might make it hard to stick to your fast.)

8. You're Pushing Yourself Too Hard.

"I've been doing IF almost 2 months, mostly OMAD, sometimes 48/72 hours extended fasts. The last 3 or 4 days whenever I break my fast I feel a great regret. I always feel like I could push the fast a little longer. What should I do?"

Extending a fast doesn't supercharge the powers of IF. If this sounds familiar to you, please find yourself a counselor who specializes in eating disorders.

I'm not saying you, or this person here, has an eating disorder, but food should not induce feelings of remorse or regret. Left untreated, this could develop into a larger problem. And also, huge kudos to this person for so bravely speaking up and sharing their food feelings!

9. Attempting to do too many things at once – over train, under eat and try fasting.

If you have spent a number of years eating badly and not exercising and you would like to try IF, don't bite off more than you can chew (pun intended!) at the start. Ease yourself into fasting and training gradually; don't start training five times per week, fasting every day and restricting calories when you do eat from day one.

The combination can lead to problems. Your body thrives with a little bit of physical stress here and there but too much stress can create chronic issues.

10. You're not drinking enough.

Your intermittent fasting regimen might have you refraining from food, but water should always be nearby, especially since you're missing out on the hydration you often get from foods like fruits and veggies. Dehydration can lead to muscle cramps, headaches, and exacerbate hunger pangs, so always make sure you're sipping H2O between (and during) feasts.

Followed all the rules and still struggling? It's not you; it's likely the diet. Research suggests that intermittent fasting has a 31 percent dropout rate, while research on diets in general suggests that as much as 95 percent of diets fail.

Try to focus more on what your body tells you, rather than what the clock says, and you're much more likely to get the nutrition your body needs.

11. Giving Up Too Soon.

Intermittent fasting takes a certain amount of discipline, but as mentioned above, it also takes time to get used to. The first four to five days are definitely the hardest. You will feel hungry.

You might feel lightheaded or exhausted or get headaches. Know that those feelings quickly pass and by the end of the first week, your body will start to adapt.

Your hunger will actually diminish and you'll start to feel more energetic and more focused. If you don't feel better after the first week, you may be doing too much too soon, or you may have chosen a plan that doesn't work for you.

How to Avoid Common Mistakes of Intermittent Fasting

Tip 1: Gradually stretch out the number of hours you go between meals until you reach a 12-hour eating window. Then move to a 10-hour eating window and reduce by small increments until you reach your goal.

Tip 2: Plan ahead. Prepare a healthy meal that's ready for you when your fast ends and make sure to eat whole ingredients when possible including healthy carbs like whole grains, lean protein and plenty of veggies, says Fung.

Tip 3: Track your hydration using an app like MyFitnessPal, which can help keep you accountable and stick to water, plain tea or black coffee while fasting.

Tip 4: "Gradually change your diet along with your eating schedule by incorporating healthier foods slowly," suggests Stephens. This prevents you from trying to overhaul everything at once, which is more sustainable.

Tip 5: Keep up with your usual workout routine or try something low-impact like walking. If you fast overnight and exercise in the morning, you can eat a protein-rich meal after, which helps you increase the rate at which you build muscle.

Tip 6: Shift your schedule forward or backward by a few hours on days when you've got plans with friends so you can still enjoy socializing. "It's a lifestyle, and it has to fit into life's special occasions," An expert says. "Intermittent fasting can be flexible."

FREQUENTLY ASKED QUESTIONS (FAQS) OF INTERMITTENT FASTING

Here are answers to the most common questions about intermittent fasting.

1. Can I Drink Liquids During the Fast?

Yes. Water, coffee, tea and other non-caloric beverages are fine. Do not add sugar to your coffee. Little amounts of milk or cream may be okay.

Coffee can be particularly beneficial during a fast, as it can dull hunger.

2. Isn't It Unhealthy to Skip Breakfast?

No. The problem is that most stereotypical breakfast captains have unhealthy lifestyles. If you make sure to eat healthy food for the rest of the day, then the practice is perfectly healthy.

3. Can I Take Supplements While Fasting?

Yes. However, keep in mind that some supplements like fat-soluble vitamins may work better when taken with meals.

4. Can I Work out While Fasted?

Yes, fasted workouts are fine. Some people recommend taking branched-chain amino acids(BCAAs) before a fasted workout. You can find many BCAA products on Amazon.

5. Will Fasting Cause Muscle Loss?

All weight loss procedures can cause muscle loss, which is why it's important to lift weights and keep your protein intake high. One study showed that intermittent fasting causes less muscle loss than regular calorie restriction.

6. Will Fasting Slow Down My Metabolism?

No. Studies show that short-term fasts actually boost metabolism. However, longer fasts of 3 or more days can overwhelm metabolism.

7. Should Kids Fast?

Allowing your child to fast is probably a bad idea.

8. Won't fasting make me hungry?

The answer is no. Most of your fast happens when you are sleeping at night. And contrary to popular belief, the fasting phase has a suppressive effect on hunger. And when you finally do break your fast, you get to eat large portions that endorse satiety (appetite satisfaction).

Oftentimes you may think you are hungry, but in actual fact, you are just thirsty. Both hunger and thirst are controlled by the hypothalamus. That explains why you often misinterpret thirst for hunger. So when you feel hungry, drink a glass of water. You can drink as much calorie free liquids as you want during your fasting phase.

9. Is Bulletproof coffee okay to consume fasted?

I do not consume coconut oil or butter in my fasted state. I am not a fan of adding coconut oil or butter to morning coffee, and this is why: Although fats have no effect on insulin, consuming these "extra calories" are not without consequence.

If you spike your coffee with butter and coconut oil (a.k.a. "bulletproof coffee"), then you must subtract ~440 calories and ~50g of fat from your calorie allowance. Failure to track these calories will result in weight gain. Furthermore, report suggests "bulletproof coffee" may be boosting hyperlipidemia in otherwise healthy folks. Consult with your physician.

10. Are there any disadvantages to fasting?

Approximately people complain of headaches and nausea when they first start fasting. For the majority of people, these signs go away after 2 weeks. As always, consult with your physician.

Be warned that fasting can really boost your energy levels and you may have trouble falling asleep, so limit your caffeine consumption to the morning and early afternoon hours only.

Be prepared to go to the bathroom frequently because of your high fluid intake during your fasts.

Be prepared to get very cold towards the end of your fast. Sometimes my fingers and toes become really cold (almost numb). When you fast, there is more blood flood travelling to your body fat, supposedly to help move it to your muscles where it can be burned as a fuel.

Because of this increased blood flow to your body fat, your vessels in your fingertips and toes vasoconstrict to compensate. So if you are cold, then rejoice! You are burning fat!

11. Will Fasting make me store fat? Will I Enter into Starvation Mode?

If you keep eating meals every two to three hours from the time you wake up until the time you go to bed, you will be chronically suppressing fat oxidation (i.e. fat burning). You will never give your body a chance to burn anything other than the food you are eating. You will have a hard time losing fat.

Fasting decreases your insulin levels. This is good because lipolysis (the process whereby your stored fat is broken down for energy) will finally be able to occur.

Key points:

- You burn fat when you are fasting.
- You burn food when you are eating.

No, your metabolism will not slow down and you will not enter into starvation mode if you fast. It is ludicrous to equate starvation with skipping breakfast or not eating for 20 hours, or even for two days! According to the American Journal of Clinical Nutrition, the earliest evidence of a lowered metabolic rate in response to fasting occurs after 60 hours (with an 8% drop in resting metabolic rate).

12. But I thought I had to eat every two to three hours to keep my blood sugar levels stable and to prevent hunger and fainting?

Why is our society convinced that shaking, light-headedness, hypoglycemia, and fainting will occur if they skip a meal, skip breakfast, or exercise fasted? Is it possible that the "perceived symptoms" of hypoglycemia are merely a result of unease over not eating? Because it's a fact that the average healthy person will not experience a drop in blood sugar while fasting. In fact, a 24-hour fast will not place you into a state of hypoglycemia.

Do you think humans could have survived on this planet if our bodies could not regulate blood sugar? As long as you are healthy, then your blood sugar levels are not going to swing wildly from one extreme to another. So no, you will not faint, feel weak, or become confused if you skip a meal or two. Your body will maintain your blood sugar levels even when you can't stuff your face with food.

Perhaps you worry that you can't hack intermittent fasting (i.e. skipping breakfast) because you are accustomed to eating from the moment you wake up until you go to bed. Naturally, you assume skipping breakfast would make you hungry.

Let me explain why eating every 2 to 3 hours is the reason why you are hungry: it's because you have trained your body to be hungry every 2 to 3 hours! The solid stream of carbs with which you are stuffing your face is suppressing your body's endogenous glucose creation. In other words, your body never needs to tap into your stored glycogen or fat for energy because you are constantly bulk energy (i.e. food) directly into your mouth. Now you've trained your body to rely on burning the food you shovel into your mouth for energy. This explains why eating carbs every few hours makes you hungry for more carbs every few hours.

Fasting, on the other hand, has a brutal effect on hunger. And when you finally do break your fast, you get to eat large portions that promote satiety (appetite satisfaction).

Remember this key point: There is always enough glycogen stored in your liver to meet your immediate energy needs. If you burn through all that stored glycogen, you won't pass out or get dizzy because your body will start breaking down fat for fuel. Good!

13. What is calorie and carb cycling?

I became quite lean when I started intermittent fasting, but I became even leaner when I started calorie and carb cycling, and introducing episodic carb refeeds. This approach prevents a decline in my metabolic rate when dieting for fat loss because I don't control my calories every single day.

Therefore, my leptin levels are not stuck in "low gear" and my body doesn't have to try to conserve calories by slowing its metabolic rate. Plus, I get to eat carbs! Don't worry, I teach you carb refeeding and how to calorie and carb cycle in my Fat Loss Fast System.

14. Can I Exercise When Intermittent Fasting?

I absolutely encourage you to practice as many different types of exercise as possible. Just like nutrition, I think variety is the key to exercise and both yoga and mountain biking are excellent examples of exercises that complement intermittent fasting.

As long as you are doing some form of resistance training at least two or three times a week you will not lose muscle since intermittent fasting actually increases development hormone, which helps preserve muscle.

One thing you may notice is if you work out on day in which you're fasting, your energy levels may be a little lower.

That's because the workout will be tapping into lowered glycogen reserves, which means you may fatigue sooner than on a traditional "eating" day.

However, exercising, especially for short durations at high intensity, in a fasted state is a furtive mace I would strongly support you to explore as it will accelerate fat loss tremendously.

15. Why Do I Get a Headache When Intermittent Fasting?

First of all, not everyone does.

But there has been a lot of research on Ramadan fasting and headaches. It seems that women are particularly susceptible to headaches while fasting.

This is not due to dehydration and may actually be similar to extraction symptoms, similar to the headaches you experience when you quit drinking coffee cold-turkey.

From my experience, if you experience headaches they do tend to go away after your first couple of fasts.

If needed, you can treat your headache as you normally would when not fasting. Just remember to drink lots of water and get some fresh air during your fast (and in general).

16. Can I Still Take My Supplements When Intermittent Fasting?

You can but I would give your body a break for the day. So if you're taking multivitamins, fish oil, probiotics, etc.... just take a day off from supplementation.

This may also help prevent your body from emerging sensitivities to commonly consumed supplements and ingredients that can occur with continued consumption of literally any food product.

17. Is Intermittent Fasting Safe for Women?

Ah, I've saved the best for last.

This is the biggest area of controversy when it comes to intermittent fasting.

Those who caution women against intermittent fasting state that studies show that it negatively impacts fertility. And that's true.

Unfortunately, what most of these people fail to realize is that ALL of these studies use "alternate day" fasting protocols where women are literally eating nothing every other day!

No wonder their hormones get messed up and have fertility issues.

Remember, I'm advising a 1-day fast – once per week – which is much, much safer and I've yet to see any negative effects in the thousands of women that I've helped with intermittent fasting.

There is some research that looked at the effect of short-term fasting on the menstrual cycle of women.

These research studies initiate that despite the metabolic changes that occur during fasting, even fasts as long as 72 hours do not seem to have an effect on the menstrual cycle of normal cycling women.

Interestingly, even longer fasts have been shown to have little impact on the menstrual cycle of normal weight women.

There is research, however, to suggest that longer fasts (72 hours) can affect the menstrual cycle of exceptionally lean women (body fat levels well below 20%).

Overall, there's a lot of research (even some of the "alternate day" studies) that show intermittent fasting to be safe, healthy, and effective at burning fat in women of all shapes and sizes.

But again, we're not going crazy with this and only fasting for no longer than 24 hours.

Nevertheless, if you're a woman and still unsure whether or not intermittent fasting is right for you, then my advice would be to inch yourself into it so that you're fasting for 8-10 hours at a time. Then gradually increase that length of time as you see fit.

CHAPTER 5 :

INTERMITTENT FASTING HACKS AND TIPS

And to help you get started on your intermittent fasting voyage, here are some great tips and tricks that'll help you stick to weight loss goals. These are ideas that are all easy to implement, have impressive results, and will make your diet plan easier. So check them out and let me know what you think!

Focus on Eating Healthy Food

After fasting for 16 hours, don't let yourself think that you can now eat anything you want. Rather, focus on eating whole foods that'll fill up your body with the important vitamins and nutrition you need. This will boost your energy and balance your hormones throughout the whole fasting period.

Avoid Artificially Flavored Drinks

Ditch the diet soda, energy drinks, and other seasoned beverages that say they're low in sugar. They actually have a lot of artificial sweeteners that are horrible for your health. They use things like Splenda or Sweet & Low which stimulate your appetite and cause you to overeat.

Drink More Water

One of the most important features in any diet plan is to make sure your body is well hydrated. By simply drinking a glass of water before each meal, the water will soothe your craving and make you feel fuller sooner (so you can avoid overeating).

Also, try adding some fresh fruit and herbs to your water for a detoxifying drink. It's tasty and totally healthy.

Keep Yourself Busy During the Fasting Hours

Whenever possible, during the fasting hours, make sure you're being busy and fruitful. Try taking a walk in the park, write in your journal, run some errands, or read your favorite book. These are just simple tricks that'll distract you from thinking about food.

Get Enough Sleep

Sleep is a vital indicator of your overall health and well-being. It helps repair your body and lose weight. And the reason for this is because our bodies burn calories while performing certain functions while sleeping and which also boosts your metabolism.

Control Your Stress

Stress can trigger overeating which makes intermittent fasting seem nearly tongue-tied to maintain. When you're influenced by stress and lack of good sleep, you'll tend to focus on eating unhealthy food to make yourself feel better. So learn to control your stress while on this diet.

Remember Fasting Means Zero

While on the intermittent fasting diet, always be true to yourself and meticulous. By simply not eating any food during the fasting hours, this will help you make sure you're losing weight at the speed you want.

Exercise

Lastly, after applying all of these tips, do yourself a favor and exercise. There's no need to enroll in a gym membership, there are plenty of workouts that can be done in the comfort of your home. They'll boost your energy, increase your muscle asset and endurance, and help your body burn fat fast.

Doing intermittent fasting shouldn't be hard or complicated. There are always plenty of tips and hacks, like the ten ideas from above that'll definitely help you out so much. Plus, they're all easy to apply and have great results. So give the diet a try and let me know what you think!

USAGE OF INTERMITTENT FASTING

1. I believe in my ability to love and accept myself for who I am.
2. I set myself free from all the guilt I carry around the food I chose in the past.
3. Every day I am exercising and taking care of my body.
4. Healing is happening in both my body and mind.
5. Every time I inhale, fresh energy fills my entire being and every time I exhale, all toxins and body fat leave my body.
6. My health is improving more and more every day, and so is my body.
7. Everything I eat heals and nourishes my body, which helps me reach the ideal weight.
8. I am closer and closer to my ideal weight with each and every day.
9. I am so happy and grateful now that I weigh _____ kilograms/pounds. (Fill in the desired number)
10. I can do this, I am doing this, my body is losing weight right now.
11. I am letting go of any guilt I hold around food.
12. Eating healthy foods helps my body get all of the nutrients it needs to be in best shape.
13. I am closer and closer to my ideal weight with each and every day.
14. I feel my desire for fat-rich foods dissolving.
15. I have a strong urge to eat only healthy foods, and let go of any processed foods.
16. I am the best version of myself, and I am working hard to become even better. I will lose weight because I want to, and I have the power to do this.
17. My body is my temple, and I attentively take care of it every day by eating only healthy foods that heal and nourish me.
18. I am aware that my metabolism is working in my advantage by helping me in gaining my optimal weight.
19. I am attaining and maintaining my desired weight.
20. I have the power to easily control my weight through a combination of healthy eating and exercising.

INTERMITTENT FASTING RECIPES

BRUNCH AND DINNER PLAN

EGG SCRAMBLE WITH SWEET POTATOES

- Overall time: **25 mins**
- Servings: **1**

INGREDIENTS:

- 1 (8-oz) positive white colored potato, diced
- 1/2 cup reduce red onion
- 2 tablespoon cut rosemary oil
- Sodium
- Pepper
- 4 big eggs
- 4 significant egg whites
- 2 tablespoon sliced chive

DIRECTIONS:

Preheat pot to 425 degrees F. Shake the interesting potato, salt, rosemary oil and reddish onion and pepper on a flat saucepan.Sprinkle with spray and roast until tender, approximately 20 minutes.

Whip the potatoes, egg whites and a splash of salt and pepper together in a station cup.

Sprinkle a fry pan with food spray preparation and scurry the agitate stations, about 5 minutes.

Spray with chives cut and serve on spud.

Every serving: 571 calories, 44 g of protein, 52 g of carbs (9 g thread), 20 g of excess fat.

CLASSICAL CHICKPEA WAFFLES TOTAL

- Overall time: **30 mins**
- Servings: **2**

INGREDIENTS:

- 3/4 cup chickpea flour
- 1/2 tbsp cooking soda
- 1/2 tablespoon sodium
- 3/4 cup ordinary 2% Greek yogurt
- 6 sizable eggs

To serve (optional), tomatoes, cucumbers, scallion, olive oil, parsley, yogurt and lemon extract. Salt, and onions.

DIRECTIONS:

Oven preheat to 200 ° F. Place a cake rack over a piece of rimmed cooking, and put it in the cooktop. Warmth of a toaster oven in every way.

Mix the flour, baking soda, and sodium into a sizable meal. In a tiny dish, combine yogurt and eggs together. Remove the damp ingredients straight into the ingredients completely dry out.

Finishing toaster gently with spray of premium ready food items. In sets, reduce the combination of 1/4 to 1/2 cup in each component of the iron and gourmet chef to 4 to 5 minutes of golden brownish. The waffles transactions to the oven, and keep them comfortable. Standard with mix of stay.

Serve waffles with a savory tomato mix, or a cozy almond butter and berries drizzle.

Every serving: 412 calories, 35 g of protein, 24 g of carbohydrates (4 g thread), 18 g of excess body fat.

PB&J Overnight Oats

- Total Time: **5 minutes** (plus 8 hours for refrigeration)
- Servings: **1**

Ingredients:

- 1/4 cup quick-cooking spun oats.
- 1/2 cup 2 per-cent dairy.
- 3 tablespoon velvety peanut butter.
- 1/4 cup mushed up raspberries.
- 3 tbsp entire raspberries.

Directions:

In a tool bowl, combine oatmeals, milk, peanut butter, and mushed up raspberries. Stir until smooth.

Cover and amazing over night. In the morning, top and uncover with entire raspberries.

Every serving: 455 calories, 20 g protein, 36 g carbohydrates (9 g thread), 28 g excess fat.

TURMERIC EXTRACT TOFU SCRAMBLE

- Complete time: **15 minutes**
- Servings: **1**

INGREDIENTS:

- 1 portobello mushroom.
- 3 or even 4 cherry tomatoes.
- 1 tbsp olive oil, plus a lot more for cleaning.
- Salt and pepper.
- 1/2 block (14-oz) agency tofu.
- 1/4 tsp ground turmeric remove.
- Dash garlic grain.
- 1/2 avocado, very finely sliced.

DIRECTIONS:

Preheat oven to 400 ° F.

Place the tomatoes and shroom on a baking sheet, and brush with oil. Sprinkle with salt and pepper. Roast for approximately 10 minutes, until tender.

Meanwhile, mix the tofu, turmeric, garlic grain and a small volume of salt into a medium dish. Mash and a fork.

Heat up 1 tbsp olive oil over low in a large saucepan.

Add the tofu mixture and cook for about 3 minutes until firm and egg-like, stirring at regular intervals.

Serve the tofu with mushroom, tomatoes and avocado and cover it.

Every serving: 431 calories, 21 g healthy protein, 17 g carbohydrates (8 g thread), 33 g fat.

<u>Avocado Ricotta Power Toast</u>

- Complete Time: **5 minutes**
- Servings: **1**

INGREDIENTS:

- 1 reduce whole-grain bread.
- 1/4 mature avocado, smashed.
- 2 tablespoon ricotta.
- Squeeze smashed reddish pepper scabs.
- Squeeze half-cracked ocean salt.

DIRECTIONS:

Prepare your breadstuffs. Best of all with mango, ricotta, broken red pepper crusts and ocean salt. Eat with rushed, even hard-boiled eggs, plus a natural yogurt serving, or even fruit piece.

Every serving: 288 calories, 10 g healthy protein, 29 g carbs (10 g thread), 17 g body fat.

TURKISH EGG BREAKFAST TOTAL

- Complete Time: **13 mins**
- Servings: **2**

INGREDIENTS:

- 2 tbsp olive oil.
- 3/4 cup diced reddish alarm system pepper.
- 3/4 cup diced eggplant.
- Press each of salt and pepper.
- 5 huge eggs, carefully knocked.
- 1/4 tablespoon paprika.
- Diced cilantro, to taste.
- 2 blobs straightforward organic yogurt.
- 1 whole-wheat pita.

DIRECTIONS:

Heat the olive oil in a medium-high, large, high-quality frying pan. Add pepper, sodium, eggplant, and pepper in the alarm. Sauce until relaxed, about 7 minutes.

Interfere with taste with the eggs, paprika and extra salt and pepper. Prep, commonly mixing up until the eggs are slightly hurried.

Sprinkle with decrease cilantro and serve with a ball of natural yogurt and the pita.

Every serving: 469 calories, 25 g healthy protein, 26 g carbohydrates (4 g thread), 29 g physical body excess fat.

ALMOND APPLE SPICE MUFFINS

- Total Time: **15 mins**
- Servings: **5**

INGREDIENTS:

- 1/2 stick butter.
- 2 cups almond food.
- 4 scoops vanilla protein particle.
- 4 sizable eggs.
- 1 cup unsweetened applesauce.
- 1 tablespoon sugar-cinnamon.
- 1 tbsp allspice.
- 1 tablespoon cloves.
- 2 tablespoon food preparation bit.

DIRECTIONS:

Preheat the cooktop to 350 ° F. In a little bit of microwave-safe bowl, dissolve the butter in the microwave on small heat, concerning 30 secs.

Mix all the remaining ingredients thoroughly with the dissolved butter.

Spray 2 bun compartments with food preparation spray or dish linings for use with nonstick food.

Put the mixture into the compartments of the muffin, ascertaining that it will not spill (3/4 full). This has 10 muffins to make.

Place one shelf in the oven and make ready for 12 minutes.

DINNER RECIPES

CHICKEN TACOS

- Total time: **25 minutes**

- Servings: **4**

INGREDIENTS:

- 2 tsp oil.
- 1 little reddish onion, cut.
- 1 clove garlic, thoroughly cut.
- 1 pound. extra-lean ground chicken.
- 1 tablespoon sodium-free taco seasonings.
- 8 whole-grain corn tortillas, warmed up.
- 1/4 cup harsh lotion.
- 1/2 cup shredded Mexican cheese.
- 1 avocado, decrease.
- Condiment, for serving.
- 1 cup hairstyle lettuce.

DIRECTIONS:

Heats up the oil in a big skillet on large outlets. Add the red onion and cook, blending for 5 to 6 mins until tender. Interfere with the garlic and beat for 1 min.

Prepare the chicken and feed it, smash it with a spoon until almost brownish, 5 minutes.

Add the seasonings with taco and 1 cup of tea.
Simmer till deducted more than half, 7 mins.

Fill out the tortillas with turkey and best with sour cream, cheese, condiment, lettuce, and avocado.

Every serving: 472 calories, 28 g of protein, 30 g of carbohydrates (6 g of fibre), 27 g of excess fat in the body.

WELL-BALANCED SPAGHETTI BOLOGNESE

- Total time: **1 hour 30 minutes**
- Servings: **4**

INGREDIENTS:

- 1 major pastas squash.
- 3 tbsp olive oil.
- 1/2 tablespoon garlic powder.
- Kosher salt and pepper.
- 1 tiny reddish onion, meticulously cut.
- 1 1/4 pound. ground chicken.
- 4 cloves garlic, finely cut.
- 8 oz. small cremini mushrooms, cut.
- 3 mugs fresh diced tomatoes (or also 2 15- oz canisters).
- 1 (8-oz) can quickly low-sodium, no-sugar- added tomato dressing.
- Fresh sliced up basil.

DIRECTIONS:

Preheat the heating to 400 ° F. Sliced pastas squash lengthwise, and get rid of seeds.

Massage every half with 1/2 tbsp of oil, and time with garlic particle and 1/4 tbsp of each salt and pepper.

Blemish skin layer atop a rimmed food

preparation item, and roast for 35 to 40 minutes until tender. Allow to cool down for 10 minutes.

However, in a significant skillet on channel, cozy remaining 2 Tbsp oil.

Add the onion, time with 1/4 tablespoon each salt and pepper, and prepare, mixing from time to time, till tender, 6 minutes.

Add the chicken and prep, split it straight into a little sacrifice a spoon, 6 to 7 minutes till it is browned. Add the garlic and prepare 1 min.

Move the mixture of chicken away from the pan, then add the mushrooms to the other. Chef, occasionally stirring, 5 mins until the mushrooms are tender. Interfere with the chicken.

Add the dressing onions and tomatoes and simmer for 10 minutes.

Take the squash as the sauce turns, and move to tables.

Spoon the Bolognese chicken over the very best and, if desired, dispersed with basil.

Every serving: 450 calories, 32 g healthy protein, 31 g carbs (6 g string), 23 g physical body fat.

CHICKEN WITH FRIED CAULIFLOWER RICE

- Total time: **35 minutes**
- Servings: **4**

INGREDIENTS:

- 2 tablespoon grapeseed oil.
- 1 1/4 pound. boneless, skinless chicken boob, attacked to likewise thickness.
- 4 significant eggs, defeated.
- 2 reddish alarm peppers, carefully sliced.
- 2 small carrots, carefully diced.
- 1 onion, very carefully diced.
- 2 cloves garlic, properly diced.
- 4 scallions, finely cut, plus much more for serving.
- 1/2 cup frozen veggies, liquefied.
- 4 mugs cauliflower "rice".
- 2 tbsp low-sodium soy products sauce.
- 2 tablespoon rice white vinegar.
- Kosher sodium and pepper.

DIRECTIONS:

Comfort 1 tablespoon of oil in a big, entrenched fry pan over medium-high.

Add the chicken and plan for 3 to 4 moments each side until golden brownish.Transfer to a reduction board and allow for the remaining 6 minutes prior to slicing. Add 1 tbsp of remaining oil into the frying pot.

Add the eggs and nationality for 1 to 2 moments, until just established; transfer to a recipe.

Add the reddish onion, carrot, and pepper and cook alarm to the fry pan, mixing regularly until tender for 4 to 5 mins.

Mix in the garlic and ready, 1 minutes. Shake with scallions and veggies.

Add the cauliflower, soya products dressing, rice vinegar, salt and

pepper and toss to mix.
After that, allow the cauliflower rest, without blending, up until starting to brownish, 2 to 3 minutes.

Shake with the sliced up chicken and eggs.
Every serving: 427 calories, 45 g healthy protein, 25 g carbs (7 g thread), 16 g excess body fat.

PIECE PAN STEAK

- Complete time: **50 mins**
- Servings: **4**

INGREDIENTS:

- 1 extra pound. littlebit of cremini mushrooms, trimmed and reduce in one- half.
- 1 1/4 lb. number broccolini, cut and reduce correct in to 2-in. lengths.
- 4 cloves garlic, properly cut.
- 3 tbsp olive oil.
- 1/4 tablespoon red pepper scabs (or also a bit additional for extra zest).
- Kosher salt and pepper.
- 2 1-in.- thick New York bit porks (about 1 1/2 lb total), reduce of excess fat.
- 1 15-oz may low-sodium cannellini surfaces, washed out.

DIRECTIONS:

Preheat to 450 ° F the cooker. Toss the mushrooms, broccolini, garlic, oil, red pepper scabs and 1/4 tsp each salt and pepper on a large rimmed preparing food sheet.

Place the piece of baking in the oven and roast for 15 mins.

Push the skillet blend sideways to showcase the meats. Time the core in the skillet facility with 1/4 table spoon each salt and pepper and place.

For medium-rare, toast the steaks to preferred doneness, 5 to 7 moments each tip.

Moving the meat products to a reduced panel and allowing 5 minutes of rest before slicing. Add the grains to the food preparation slab and toss to include.

109

Roast until heated via, around 3 mins. Serve surfaces and vegetables with steak.

Every serving: 464 calories, 42 g healthy protein, 26 g carbs (8 g thread), 22 g body system excess fat.

PORK TENDERLOIN WITH SQUASH BUTTERNUT AND BRUSSELS SPROUTS

- Total time: **50 min**
- Servings: **4**

INGREDIENTS:

- 1 3/4 pound. pig tenderloin, trimmed.
- Sodium.
- Pepper.
- 3 tbsp canola oil.
- 2 sprigs fresh thyme.
- 2 garlic cloves, peeled off.
- 4 mugs Brussels sprouts, trimmed and cut in half.
- 4 mugs diced butternut squash.

DIRECTIONS:

Heat up the device to 400 ° F. Season the tenderloin all over with salt and pepper. Heat energy 1 taste of oil higher over channel in a large cast iron skillet. Once the oil glows, sear and spread the tenderloin on all sides for 8 to 12 minutes until gold gray. On to a side.

Add the thyme and garlic to the frying pan and stay 2 tbsp of oil, and chef for about 1 min, until odor is great.

Fasten the sprouts in Brussels, squash with butternut and each sprinkle with a big salt and pepper. Prepare, mix regularly, for 4 to 6 moments, until the vegetables are a little brown.

Find the tenderloin on top of the vegetables, and transmit to the oven every little thing. Roast until the injured vegetables and a meat product thermostat put right into the thickest part of the tenderloin shows 140 ° F, 15 to 20 minutes.

Use cooktop gloves to remove the frying pan from the stove altogether.

Before the veggies go up and serve, enable the tenderloin to rest about 5 minutes. Shake for edge feature with a vinaigrette dressing, eco-friendly.

Each serving: 401 calories, 44 g healthy protein, 25 g carbohydrates (6 g thread), 15 g body system excess fat.

WILD CAJUN SPICED SALMON

- Total time: **30 mins**
- Servings: **4**

INGREDIENTS:

- 1 1/2 lb. untamed Alaskan salmon fillet.
- Sodium-free taco seasoning.
- 1/2 scalp cauliflower (regarding 1 lb), separated flowers.
- 1 scalp broccoli (concerning 1 extra pound), separated florets.
- 3 tablespoon olive oil.
- 1/2 tablespoon garlic grain.
- 4 units. Tomatoes, diced.

DIRECTIONS:

Preheat oven to 375 ° F. Put the salmon in a saucepan. In a little dish, combine the taco seasoning with 1/2 cup water. Area the mixture over the salmon, and bake till cloudy for 12 to 15 minutes.

Pulse the cauliflower and cabbage in a food stuff cpu potato chip (in sets as needed), until properly cut and "riced". The oil warms up in a huge frying pan on the tool. Add the cauliflower and broccoli, scattered with garlic bit, and the chef, tossing for 5 to 6 moments until only tender.

Serve salmon besides "rice" and finest with tomatoes.

For every serving: 408 calories, 42 g of protein, 9 g of carbohydrates (3 g of thread), 23 g of fat.

PORK CHOPS WITH BLOODY MARY TOMATO SALAD

- Complete time: **25 minutes**
- Servings: **4**

INGREDIENTS:

- 2 tablespoon olive oil.
- 2 tablespoon reddish white wine white colored vinegar.
- 2 tbsp Worcestershire sauce.
- 2 tablespoon ready horseradish, pressed completely dry.
- 1/2 tsp Tabasco.
- 1/2 tablespoon oats seeds.
- Kosher salt.
- 1 pint cherry tomatoes, halved.
- 2 oats stems, really very finely cut.
- 1/2 tiny reddish onion, very finely sliced.
- 4 tiny bone-in pig chops (1 in. slow-witted, involving 2 1/4 lb total amount).
- Pepper.
- 1/4 cup carefully diced flat-leaf parsley.
- 1 little scalp green-leaf lettuce, leaves behind torn.

DIRECTIONS:

Accurate to lead bigger barbecue. In a big tub, whip the butter, white vinegar, Worcestershire sauce, horseradish, Tabasco, celery seeds and 1/4 tbsp salt together. Shake the tomatoes, onion, and oatmeal with it.

Season the pig chops with 1/2 tablespoon of each sodium and pepper, grill until perfectly browned, and prepare 5 to 7 minutes per edge just through.

Fold the parsley right in to the tomatoes and serve over the veggies and pig. Eat with chopped cauliflower and even white potatoes.

For every serving: 400 calories, 39 g of protein, 8 g of carbs, 23 g of bod.

CONCLUSION

With intermittent fasting becoming more and more popular as a weight-loss and health management diet, it is important to understand how to set it up; here are three keys to make sure that you can get involved in an intermittent fasting lifestyle as soon as possible.

Intermittent fasting doesn't need to be a short term approach to dieting and is in fact much more successful as a genuine lifestyle choice. The first decision to make therefore is how to adapt a fast to YOUR life. Remember that the fast can be anywhere from 16 hours to several days in length depending on exactly what you are trying to accomplish. The two approaches that are perhaps easiest to set up are an alternating day (24 hour) fast/eat cycle, or a 16/8 cycle.

When do I work out? This question is key. Diet is with doubt the most important factor in weight-loss and good health, but to really get the best out of an intermittent fast, the re-feed should coincide with your workout. Personally, I have had good success with a fast from 8Pm until the next day at lunch and an early afternoon training session. All the food that I am taking in around my workout is being used for fuel and to repair muscle rather than being stocked as body-fat.

What do I want to accomplish with intermittent fasting? Is your aim fat-loss, muscle gain, enhanced health or a combination of all three? Depending on your answer to these questions, you can start to identify exactly how long your fast should be and what quantity of food you should be eating during the eating "window".

A SPECIAL GIFT FOR YOU

As I promised, by purchasing this book you will receive a special gift: **the airfryer cookbook**, that I wrote for you to enjoy also fried foods, without sacrificing your health! Write me "I want the airfryer cookbook" here: kimberly.rylie@gmail.com

Well, now you're ready to become the best version of yourself! I hope that you enjoyed this guide and I'd really love to hear your thoughts. Please, let me know with a short review, it means a lot to me!

Thanks for your time!

Printed in Great Britain
by Amazon